# EASY-CARE
## LANDSCAPE PLANS

### 41 Professional Designs For Do-It-Yourselfers

*Created by*
**Susan A. Roth & Company**

*Landscape Designs by*
**Ireland-Gannon Associates, Inc.**

*Project Managers:*
**Michael J. Opisso & Damon Scott**

*Landscape Illustrations by*
**Ray Skibinski**

**HOME PLANNERS, INC.**
Tucson, Arizona

Designed and Produced by: SUSAN A. ROTH & COMPANY
3 Lamont Lane
Stony Brook, NY 11790

Publisher: Susan A. Roth
Associate Editor: Pam Peirce
Copy Editor: Lynn McGowan
Writers: Susan Lang and Susan A. Roth
Irrigation Consultant: Robert Kourik

Landscape designs by: Ireland-Gannon, Associates, Inc.
Rt. 25A, Northern Blvd.
East Norwich, NY 11732

Designers: Jeffrey Diefenbach, Edward D. Georges, Salvatore A. Masullo, James E. Morgan,
Maria Morrison, Tom Nordloh, Michael J. Opisso, David Poplawski, Damon Scott

Regional Consultants:
Northeast: Carol Howe
Mid-Atlantic: Michael J. Opisso
Deep South: Nancy Jacobs Roney
Midwest: Alan Branhagen
Florida & Gulf Coast: Robert Haehle
Rocky Mountains: Allen M. Wilson
Northern California & Pacific Northwest: Jo Wilson Greenstreet
Southern California & Desert Southwest: Judith Ratliff

Artwork:
Landscape renderings: Ray Skibinski
Landscape plot plans: Damon Scott and Michael Iragorri
How-to artwork: Gary Palmer and Ron Hildebrand

*All photographs by Susan A. Roth except for:*
*David Poplawski (pages 13 and 141).*

*Cover Photo: Landscape Design by Conni Cross, Landscape Designer, Cutchogue, NY*

Published by: HOME PLANNERS, INC.
3275 West Ina Rd.
Suite 110
Tucson, Arizona 85741

President & Publisher: Rickard D. Bailey
Publications Manager: Cindy Coatsworth
Senior Editor: Paulette Mulvin
Graphic Designers: Paul Fitzgerald and Kellie Gibson

First printing August, 1995

Library of Congress Catalogue Card Number: 95-075833
ISBN softcover 1-881955-22-2
ISBN hardcover 1-881955-26-5

712.6
EAS
1995

# Contents

# Introduction

The grounds surrounding your home are your family's private outdoor living space—a space that can be arranged to be both beautiful and easy to care for. This book will help you bring out your yard's potential to become a lovely retreat, a special place to enjoy outdoor hobbies and gardening activities, or an inviting spot for outdoor entertaining and relaxing. And you'll find out how to design your property so it requires a minimum of maintenance and upkeep! You'll learn time-saving ways to perform those necessary chores that you can't avoid, so that your new low-maintenance landscape will be even easier to care for.

*Easy-Care Landscape Plans* is an unusual book. Here you will find plot plans and illustrations of professionally designed front and backyards for which you can order actual customized blueprints. You can choose to order a full-size, six-page blueprint package complete with a regionalized plant list selected for your area of the country, or use what you learn and see here as an inspiration for creating your own distinctive landscape.

This unique book is the result of the collaboration of three companies that are well-respected in their fields: Home Planners, Inc., architects and publishers of blueprints for do-it-yourself home builders and contractors; Susan A. Roth & Company, a horticultural publishing and book packaging company; and Ireland-Gannon Associates, Inc., a nationally recognized, award-winning, landscape design-build firm.

Home Planners, Inc., founded in 1946, has published over 135 books of home plans and sold more than 3 million blueprints for their designs. Their home plans are featured regularly in special issues

of *House Beautiful, Better Homes and Gardens, Colonial Homes,* and other leading shelter magazines. Their other books of landscape plans are *The Home Landscaper,* which offers designs for 40 front-yard landscapes and 15 backyards; and *The Backyard Landscaper,* which features 40 backyard designs.

Susan A. Roth & Company created *Easy-Care Landscape Plans* for Home Planners and has put together many popular gardening books for Ortho Books. The author of *The Weekend Garden Guide—Work-Saving Ways to a Beautiful Backyard* (Rodale Press, 1991) and *The Four-Season Landscape* (Rodale Press, 1994), and a contributor to many publications, Susan Roth is also a widely published garden photographer who maintains a large slide library.

Ireland-Gannon Associates, Inc., has been serving the prestigious North Shore of Long Island since

1943. In 1978, the company formed an association with the acclaimed Martin Viette Nursery, a major horticultural center in the Northeast. Ireland-Gannon has been honored with over 80 awards in the last 25 years, including several Grand Awards from the Associated Landscape Contractors of America and Superior Awards from the National Landscape Association.

By using the designs in the book, you'll have no need to hire a landscape architect or designer to create a design for you. Most top-notch firms, such as Ireland-Gannon Associates, Inc., charge between $500 and $1,000 just to design the planting scheme for a half-acre property. For a fraction of that cost, you can order a large professional-quality blueprint package tailored to your needs. Each package comes in eight regionalized versions featuring planting schemes coded with plants that are specially selected to thrive in various parts of the country. (See page 154.)

## About the Designs in This Book

In this book, horticulturists and landscape designers have combined their talents to create 41 professional-quality, easy-care landscape designs for the do-it-yourselfer and landscape contractor. The plans offer a range of possibilities for both small and large families, and for compact and spacious lots. For your convenience, the plans are divided into two chapters. Chapter 3 contains front-yard designs and Chapter 4 contains backyard designs.

Because many people have difficulty imagining what a one-dimensional planting plan will look like in reality, a full-color illustration accompanies each plot plan. These paintings show the landscape after it has matured and filled in, to give you a sense of the mood and feeling the landscape design will create a few years after installation.

In Chapter 1, you can read about how to design an easy-care landscape without sacrificing its beauty. All low-maintenance landscapes have these features in common: They use plants requiring little attention from you; their lawns are small, with few edges to trim; and the trees and shrubs are slow-growing or dwarf types that fit into the landscape without requiring regular pruning. Reading this first chapter will help you appreciate the intentions of the designs in the following chapters, and will guide

you if you create your own design from scratch.

In Chapter 2, you'll read about the easiest ways to take care of your landscape. If you want to have a beautiful property but don't have a lot of time to devote to it, you can reduce the time you spend tending it by using these tried-and-true methods. You'll learn the fastest and easiest ways to care for your landscape, including the best ways to mow a lawn and handle autumn leaves, and how to prune shrubs to slow down their growth rather than speed it up.

## How to Use This Book

The first chapter of this book provides a mini-lesson on designing for low maintenance. You'll read about the design principles that professional landscapers put into practice. Chapters 3 and 4 are the heart of the book and include the plot plans and illustrations of the designs. When you study them, you'll see how the principles discussed in Chapter 1 are used to create truly useful and attractive, easy-care landscapes.

If you would like to install any of these landscapes on your own property, use the plot plan provided in the book to guide you, modifying it, if necessary, to fit the exact contours of your house and property. The blueprint package for each design, offered separately, is helpful since it contains an enlarged, easy-to-use blueprint, a regionalized plant list selected especially for your climate, as well as several pages of

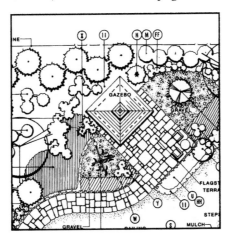

information on planting and caring for your new landscape.

Chapter 5 tells you how to work with the landscape plans shown in this book and helps you through the installation process, whether you choose to do the work yourself or hire a landscape contractor to do the planting and construction.

Chapter 6 contains large illustrations of some of the structures featured in the landscape plans, such as gazebos, swings, tool sheds, and decks. You can order building plans for any of these structures if you want to build them yourself. (See page 152 for ordering information.)

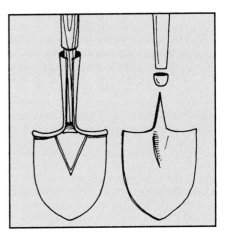

## Installing the Landscape

Most do-it-yourselfers can install any of these landscapes themselves. If you don't want to do the planting or construction yourself, you can hire a landscape contractor—a professional installer—to do the job. Keep in mind that most landscape contractors are not skilled designers, even though they may advertise themselves as such. They are skilled at maintaining a lawn, planting or removing trees, or regrading the land, but when it comes to actual landscape design, their talents may be limited. By using one of the plans in this book—whether you install it yourself or hire a contractor to do it—you can be assured that you are getting a top-quality design, one created by an award-winning landscape design firm. Landscaping is an investment in the enjoyment and value of your home, so why not begin with the best design possible?

# CHAPTER 1

# Designing For Easy Care

*With a Little Planning, You Can Have a Beautiful Yard That's a Breeze to Maintain*

Design: Conni Cross

A luxuriant, colorful landscape can be one of the most gratifying aspects of home ownership, but not if you're too busy mowing grass, raking leaves, pruning overgrown shrubs, and doing innumerable other tasks to enjoy it. Your home's landscape should improve your surroundings and increase the value of your property without making you a slave to its needs. If yard work keeps you from tennis, biking trips, or other weekend activities, then that gorgeous landscape and expansive lawn may not be worth the trouble, and some rethinking is in order.

Fortunately, an easy-care landscape that allows you greater freedom can be just as attractive and interesting as one needing high maintenance—if it's properly planned and the plants are well chosen. Low maintenance needn't be synonymous with large expanses of gravel interspersed with boulders. You don't have to go to the extreme of eliminating all plants, paving over the yard, or rolling out artificial turf to free yourself from an overwhelming amount of yard care. It just takes proper planning and a good design.

Ease of care isn't necessarily related to the size of a property. A tiny yard can require high maintenance, while a large one can be easy to care for. The difference lies in the design and plant selection. A successful easy-care landscape doesn't happen by accident; it's planned from the start. The trick is to design the yard so that you minimize—or even eliminate—routine and repetitive, time-consuming tasks, such as mowing, raking, watering, fertilizing, and grooming, while still retaining an attractive planting that enhances your home.

Some people claim that easy-care gardens take care of themselves, but that's an exaggeration. "Easy care" means just that: easy to take care of, but not effortless. You—or someone you hire—has to do some maintenance. Since "easy" is a relative term, you should decide from the outset how much time and effort—or money—you're willing to devote to yard maintenance.

Some styles of landscapes or types of plants entail more routine work than others. Figure out how many hours you can spend weekly or monthly on maintenance, and see whether that tallies generally with the needs of the particular type of landscape you're considering. For instance, you may have to clean up a naturalistic woodland only once a year to keep it attractive, while a yard featuring a lawn and perennial beds may require several hours each week to keep it in good form.

This foundation planting provides an abundance of color from easy-care plants. Hydrangea shrubs produce an explosion of shocking pink flowers in midsummer; the blossoms dry in place and remain attractive through autumn. Contrasting nicely with the lawn, purple-leaf ajuga makes an eye-catching groundcover. Impatiens—one of the easiest annuals to care for—blooms from summer until hard frost.

Design: Ireland-Gannon Associates

*A formal landscape design creates an impressive entrance to this contemporary home. The landing and broad stone steps balance the size of the house and complement the architecture. Trees and shrubs are underplanted with groundcover in mulched beds so the beds remain neat and weed-free. Easy-care spring bulbs and summer perennials provide a changing scene.*

Almost any kind of garden can be made easy care, so don't settle for something you don't really want for the sake of low maintenance. Whether renovating an existing landscape or installing a new one, you can plan for low maintenance by considering the needs of the various features in your landscape.

Here's how the different elements of a landscape rank in order of maintenance requirements, from the *least* care to the *most* care:

- Paving and other hard surfaces
- Ornamental trees and shrubs
- Groundcovers
- Informal hedges
- Flowering perennials
- Formal hedges
- Annual flowers
- Lawn

The professionally designed landscape plans in this book are attractive and colorful throughout the year, even though they are designed for low maintenance. You can achieve the same results if you rely on the pros' experience and knowledge.

## Deciding on a Style

To many homeowners, landscaping means heading to the nursery in search of pretty plants and filling the yard with them. That haphazard method may work for some, but it's risky for anyone whose goal is a low-maintenance landscape. Plant-crazy landscapers who ignore style usually take on more work than they intended. They're pushovers for every good-looking plant they see, regardless of its maintenance needs, and they end up constantly rearranging the plants, which never look quite right together.

Style simply refers to the character of the landscape—for example, whether it's a woodsy grove, a soothing expanse of green, or a happy jumble of flowers. Picking a style at random isn't any better than choosing plants indiscriminately, so choose carefully. Identifying your goals helps you settle on a style that works for you. Ask yourself what you want from the landscape. A lush green setting for your home? A place to entertain? A merging of indoors and outdoors? A fanciful escape from daily life? A bird sanctuary? A hodge-podge of flowers leading to a vine-covered cottage? A tropical paradise?

When choosing a style, remember to think beyond your own needs and tastes. The best landscapes suit their setting: They're compatible with the region, the growing con-

ditions, and the architecture of the house. A moist birch woodland is a fine choice for a Cape Cod home in New Hampshire, and a dry desert garden suits an adobe house in Arizona, but interchanging those landscapes would be ludicrous.

The smaller the lot, the more important it is to stick to a single style. On an expansive property, it's possible to have several styles as long as they don't clash visually. For example, you could have a verdant park-like setting out front and a series of decks extending from the back of the house and overlooking a natural woodland at the outer reaches of the yard. Or you may want a tidy shrub border on public view and a more informal cottage garden in the backyard.

### Formal Versus Informal

The degree of formality in a landscape heavily influences the amount of upkeep required—the more formal the yard, the more work you'll have to put into it, because neatness and order are primary to the style. Pay close attention to the characteristics of each type of landscape, and avoid strict formality if you ever want to relax on weekends.

A strictly formal landscape is easy to recognize because its struc-

*This informal design features rough-hewn stone steps that carve a curving path to the front door. The naturalistic appearance comes from using an assortment of low shrubs on the hillside; a wood-chip mulch prevents weeds and erosion. Because a naturalistic scene need not be neat as a pin to look good, the home-owners spend very little time on maintenance.*

ture—straight lines and geometric shapes—is so obvious. Trees and shrubs are commonly planted in rows, and flowers are planted in square or rectangular beds. Formal beds can also be curving, but the shape is uniformly circular or oval rather than freeform. There is a high degree of symmetry—for example, a feature on one side of a walkway is repeated on the other side. Hedges are sheared, and shrubs are often clipped into such shapes as balls, cones, and pyramids. The whole landscape has a carefully manicured look.

Obviously, a very formal garden is at odds with the concept of easy care, since there's no place for even a sprig of wayward growth or a speck of debris. Plants must be wrestled under control, weeds banished, and leaves swept away to avoid any hint of disorder.

An informal yard is just as well planned as a formal one, but its structure isn't as apparent, and there's less emphasis on order and uniformity. It is characterized by irregular shapes and curving lines, which may follow the natural contours of the terrain. Plants are often arranged in irregular masses (called drifts) instead of being lined up in rows. Trees and shrubs are allowed

to grow naturally rather than pruned into contrived shapes. A good informal design is visually balanced without being symmetrical. For example, a large shrub on one side of a walkway balances a grouping of smaller shrubs on the other side.

## Going Natural

The most informal type of landscape is a naturalistic one, which mimics nature without necessarily recreating it faithfully. Meadow and woodland gardens (see below and page 10) are two common types; others include water gardens with ponds and waterfalls, and rock gardens with alpine plants. Such landscapes usually feature plants that spread on their own by naturalizing (establishing themselves by reseeding or by vigorously spreading roots).

Informal gardens, especially naturalistic ones, are much easier to maintain than their more formal counterparts, mainly because plants in them can grow naturally and require less coddling and cleanup. A cottage garden is supposed to be a jumble of plants, some of them sprawling, jammed together, or festooned with seed heads. A woodland garden is supposed to be littered with fallen leaves and dead twigs. And a prairie garden is sup-

posed to be a sea of grasses and wildflowers punctuated by spent seed stalks and dry foliage.

***Designing a Meadow Garden*** This type of naturalistic mingling of wildflowers and bunch grasses is suitable for a large, open, sunny site. Meadow gardens are in vogue because they look so casual and are supposedly easy to maintain, yet are alive with color and movement. It's true that a meadow gets by with only a once-a-year mowing—but only after careful soil preparation, installation, watering, and weeding to get it established. Contrary to popular opinion, you can't just sprinkle a can of wildflower seeds on a languishing lawn or bramble-filled hillside and transform the site into a beautiful wildflower meadow.

Begin by clearing the soil of vegetation and making a planting bed of it. You'll save yourself work in the long run by tilling and watering the bed, waiting for the weed seeds in the soil to germinate, and killing the weed seedlings before planting the meadow. (See pages 40-42 for more on weed control.)

Some meadow mixes contain only flowers, although real meadows also have grasses. (These grasses, unlike most lawn grasses, grow in bunches

*A meadow garden consisting of native grasses and wildflowers mimics a natural site and makes a good low-maintenance alternative to a lawn on a large treeless property. The key is to plant the meadow properly and get it established. After that, the only care needed is annual mowing.*

atively well-behaved, pretty weeds such as Queen Anne's lace or goldenrod to remain, but get rid of aggressive ones such as field bindweed or Johnsongrass before they take hold. Once the meadow establishes itself, it should be dense enough to shade out invaders.

Annual mowing is important. If you don't mow, the meadow will probably revert to the vacant-lot look, with a lot of tree and shrub seedlings growing in an unrecognizable tangle of plants. Use the mower to cut paths through the meadow so that you can stroll through it and enjoy the plants up close.

A caveat before planting a meadow garden: Check local ordinances to make sure a meadow—especially one that will be in public view—is permissible. If your neighbors object, explain to them that you're growing wildflowers and that you have not simply stopped mowing. A wild garden may look more acceptable if confined by a rustic fence or used as a large border, as shown in the design on page 108.

***Designing a Woodland Shade Garden***
A woodland garden is a natural choice for any property containing a grove of trees endemic to woods or forests. It offers the virtues of quiet beauty and ease of care. Woodlands are, by definition, untidy—they're strewn with leaf litter, tree stumps, mossy logs, and rock outcroppings.

In natural woodlands, the protective branches provide shelter for several tiers of plants—understory trees, shrubs, ferns, wildflowers, and groundcovers—that flourish in the shade. You can mimic nature by layering appropriate shade-loving plants beneath your grove.

Once established, a woodland garden is easy to maintain, but getting it to that state can take a little work, depending on the condition of your grove. If it's overrun with brambles and poison ivy or poison oak, begin by getting rid of the unwelcome brush. Such aggressive undergrowth may be native to woods in your area, but you should make it your goal to mimic only the finer aspects of nature.

Clear the land, but don't cultivate as you would for a planting bed. The less digging you do, the better,

instead of forming competitive runners.) If you can't find a mix containing both types of plants, buy separate wildflower and bunch grass mixes. Check with your local native plant society about regional, or even subregional, mixes suitable for your growing area.

As an alternative, follow the example of the Backyard Meadow Gar-

den (see page 108): Plant container-grown perennials and sow native bunch grass seeds around them. This method overcomes the failure of many wildflower mixes to germinate or the flowers to reseed and return the next year.

Weeds pose a real problem in meadow gardens the first year, so keep after them. You can allow rel-

*Shady sites can be beautiful when planted with native woodland wildflowers. If grown in rich moist soil, the woodland plants spread into lush drifts. A woodland garden needs little maintenance, since fallen leaves decay naturally and actually improve plant health.*

since you don't want to disturb tree roots. As you scoop out soil for each plant, take care to avoid large roots.

Keep new plantings well watered until they're established. After that, you won't need to water much, since the plant roots will be in the cool shade. In fact, in some areas, it is not wise to irrigate near trees. In coastal California, for instance, watering under native oaks may kill the trees, so landscapers there are advised to plant drought-tolerant species just before the rainy season.

You won't have to do much training or staking of plants in a woodland shade garden, since floppy, drooping growth only contributes to the garden's charm. You won't have to worry about pulling every weed either, since weeds aren't as noticeable here as they are in a more formal setting.

The most natural-looking paths are simple mulched ones. Don't use any edgings or stepping-stones unless you can make them look as if they were created by nature.

Your woodland garden will soon be littered with leaves forming a natural mulch. Whether you have to do any raking depends on how well the leaves break down. At worst, you may have to rake tough leaves off

plants. Some woodland gardeners rake most of the fallen leaves, chop them, and then return them to the site as a fine-textured mulch. This extra step beautifies the garden, but is not necessary. (See page 47 for more guidance on shredding leaves into mulch.)

### Pleasing Yourself

Having a style in mind makes it easier to design your landscape and to select appropriate types of plants. The style gives your landscape an identity; otherwise, it would look like a random collection of flora.

Of course, the style you select should reflect your personal taste. After all, a landscape is a long-term investment that should provide you with satisfaction for many years. What good is a woodland that's a snap to maintain if you prefer something more citified? Or what does it matter that your cottage garden was designed for easy care if you prefer a more orderly setting? Above all, you must please yourself.

## Wise Landscape Plant Choices

You'll be using many types of plants to create a pleasing, interest-filled landscape. With low maintenance in mind, here's what to look for and what to avoid in each category:

*Trees with small leaves or leaflets, such as honey locust, are easy to clean up after because the fallen leaves shrivel and are easily disposed of. Some honey locusts have vicious thorns and drop long, messy pods. 'Sunburst,' pictured here, doesn't produce thorns or pods, so is easy to care for.*

*By choosing disease-resistant types of plants, you can reduce your maintenance chores considerably. Shown here is a dwarf species of lilac,* Syringa microphylla, *which is not bothered by disfiguring mildew, as are common lilacs.*

## Easy-Care Trees

Trees contribute enormously to a landscape, and they usually take a long time to grow, so choose wisely. There's no sense in planting a tree and struggling with it for several years, if you end up having to replace it because you located it too close to the house or in the wrong exposure.

Select well-behaved ornamental trees that serve a particular function. For example, they might provide shade, make a good screen, bear colorful flowers, or reveal a dramatic silhouette in winter. The trees you choose shouldn't depend on pruning to look good, or be bothered by pests or diseases that might visit your garden. Also, look for trees with strong wood that won't break in storms.

Needleleaf evergreen trees (conifers) such as pine, fir, and spruce have fine-textured needles and horizontally tiered branches that give them a graceful appearance. Broadleaf evergreen trees such as live oak and Southern magnolia are usually round-headed. The needles and leaves of evergreens do not last forever, however. Most conifers shed their oldest leaves every fall, leaving the youngest ones behind to carry on the greenery in winter. These needles are usually easy to clean up and often can be left on the ground beneath the tree to create an attractive weed-smothering mulch. Most broadleaf evergreens drop a few leaves continually and don't require a major cleanup effort.

Conifers usually grow quite large over the years and don't respond well to pruning, so be sure to site them properly. Dwarf or slow-growing types may be the best choice, but even these may eventually grow too large after many years. When that happens, it's time to renovate.

Deciduous trees usually pose more of a cleanup problem in autumn, when the leaves change color and drop. Trees with small leaflets, such as the thornless honey locust, are usually easiest to clean up after; the leaves break apart into individual leaflets that shrivel and blow away or are easily disposed of. Avoid trees that drop messy nuts or seedpods, such as horse chestnut and

*Replacing large areas of lawn with no-mow groundcovers can transform a high-maintenance property into a low-maintenance one. Trees, shrubs, and even perennials can be planted in the groundcovers to create a garden effect.*

catalpa. They may be lovely to look at when in bloom, but they make a continual mess.

## Easy-Care Shrubs

Undemanding shrubs with handsome foliage, pretty flowers, or colorful fruit are the backbone of an easy-care landscape. The key is to let them take their natural form and not make more work for yourself by pruning them into formal shapes. (For more on pruning methods, see page 42.)

Dense evergreen shrubs used as screens provide year-round privacy and cut down on leaf litter. Needled evergreens, such as junipers and yews, don't produce showy flowers, but they do offer lovely texture and dependable year-round greenery. Broadleaf evergreens, such as rhododendrons, mountain laurels, and hollies, usually have showy flowers or attractive fruits.

Deciduous shrubs, such as viburnum, provide privacy in summer. In winter, their bare limbs often make interesting silhouettes. Many put on dazzling displays of floral color in spring or summer and showy foliage and beautiful clusters of berries in fall. Go for shrubs that stay compact and tidy without pruning. And be sure to choose improved pest-resistant cultivars or types that aren't prone to problems.

## Easy-Care Groundcovers and Vines

Groundcovers play an important role in low-maintenance landscapes. Besides dressing up a landscape, they provide a weed-smothering blanket of stems and foliage, and can replace a lawn if planted close together.

To be a successful groundcover, a plant must grow thickly and quickly. When choosing plants that spread naturally over the ground, look for types that grow densely but not rampantly. The ones you pick should also provide the color, texture, and appearance you want in your landscape. In small, tidy gardens, avoid planting groundcovers such as English ivy that grow so aggressively that they quickly become a nuisance by invading areas where you never intended them to be.

Even well-behaved groundcovers need to be trimmed back occasionally.

*Flowering perennials create a changing display of colorful blossoms from spring through fall, but they can require a lot of attention. If you choose easy-care, disease-free types, such as the coneflowers, sedum, and fountain grass shown here, your landscape will boast a sea of flowers throughout summer and fall. To care for these plants, all you need do is to cut off the dried tops and remove the debris once a year in fall or late winter.*

Design: Ireland-Gannon Associates

Edgings (see pages 23-24) keep most types in bounds, although not vining sorts like periwinkle that grow right over the edging and root on the other side. Restrict rambunctious groundcovers to bare hillsides or other large areas that you want to blanket quickly. When planting on slopes, use types with deeply anchored, creeping roots to hold the soil in place. When putting groundcovers under trees, choose those that are loose enough to absorb fallen leaves, such as pachysandra. In mild-winter climates, select evergreen types to keep the landscape attractive all year.

Know how a vine climbs before you position it to scurry up your house or along a fence—some types are easier to take care of than others. Choose vines such as honeysuckle that twine their way up, or others such as porcelain vine that use tendrils to ascend. Those that use thorns to prop themselves up, like bougainvillea, or that make progress by mounding, like star jasmine, must be tied in place to train them to grow where you want them. Think before planting vines with suction disks, such as Boston ivy and Virginia creeper, or those with aerial rootlets, such as English ivy and climbing hydrangea. These vines attach so tenaciously that they can loosen clapboards and damage mortar. Getting them off surfaces you want to repaint

*Bulbs such as tulips provide beautiful flowers in early spring, but die to the ground by summer, leaving bare spots behind. By planting bulbs among later-flowering perennials, you can prevent the bare spots and hide withering bulb foliage. This saves labor since you need not cut off the yellowing leaves.*

is no easy task—they are best allowed to scale tree trunks, not buildings.

Some plants, including English ivy, winter creeper, and bougainvillea, can be used as both ground-covers and vines. To keep English ivy from running rampant, look for the smaller, slower-growing, more delicate-leafed types that are often sold as houseplants.

**Easy-Care Lawn Grass**
The various lawn grasses differ in such traits as wear resistance and tolerance to cold, heat, drought, diseases, and shade. Choose a grass type that does well in your climate but will also serve your needs. For instance, if the lawn will bear high traffic, it should be a wear-resistant type.

Keep in mind that many grass cultivars are better adapted to certain conditions than the plain-vanilla species, and thus reduce overall maintenance. Your local nursery or county agricultural extension agent should be able to advise you.

**Easy-Care Flowers**
These fleshy-stemmed plants, which include annuals, biennials, perennials, and bulbs, provide much of the color in high-maintenance gardens. But easy-care gardeners need not forgo floral color if they choose wisely.

Avoid plants that demand special care such as staking or frequent di-

vision, or that are likely to fall prey to insects or diseases. Don't bother with types that are hard to grow, and limit the number that require deadheading (removal of spent flowers) to keep blooming. Flowers that spread on their own by reseeding or naturalizing may be too invasive for some gardens, but they're usually good choices for naturalistic landscapes.

Here's an overview of the various types of herbaceous flowers:

***The Easiest Annuals*** Annuals are flowering plants that live for only one growing season. There's nothing like annuals for a long show of color, since they usually bloom nonstop for months on end if you care for them properly. But that's the trouble—they usually demand a lot of care and must be replanted every year. Most types need to be deadheaded every few days to promote continual blooming—and that means extra work. A few easy-care annuals, such as impatiens and sweet alyssum, don't need deadheading to put on a good show and therefore make excellent choices for low-maintenance landscapes.

In any event, annuals only keep growing and blooming as long as conditions are favorable. Some types, such as calendulas, grow best in cool weather; others, such as zin-

nias, prefer heat. Most annuals need plenty of water and fertilizer to do their best.

For an easy-care garden, choose annuals from the list on the opposite page and site them according to their cultural preferences. These accommodating plants flourish without deadheading, staking, or any special care, so you can enjoy their splashy flowers without much effort. All that's required is yearly planting in spring and removal of dead plants in fall.

***Long-Lived Perennials*** Perennials can live for many years, usually flowering for a few weeks each year. Many kinds have beautiful foliage that adds months of color and texture to the garden even after their flowers fade. Even though perennials survive from year to year, their tops usually die to the ground with the onset of cold, then reappear when the weather warms up. In mild-winter climates, many perennials are evergreen.

Some types, such as hosta and red-hot-poker plant, thrive in one place for many years with very little care; others are more demanding. Garden chrysanthemums, for instance, must be dug up and divided every few years because the middle of the plant dies out as the clump enlarges.

Many of the landscape designs in this book include an assortment of perennials. Some designs feature numerous perennials planted in large drifts. You need not worry that these landscapes demand a lot of care; the perennials were chosen because they bloom for a long period without deadheading, live many years without division, and flourish without staking. All you'll need to do is cut back their dead tops each year in fall or late winter.

*Best Bulbs* Most bulbous plants lie dormant underground most of the year. They send up shoots and blossoms for a short time, then disappear underground. And they usually live for many years, spreading into ever more dramatic clumps. For easy care, grow only types that can be left in place and will come back year after year. Some bulbs, such as daffodils and crocuses, naturalize under good growing conditions, forming ever-bigger clumps. Although extremely popular, hybrid tulips are iffy choices for easy-care gardens, since they tend to peter out after the first year or two and may need to be replanted each year for a dependable show.

To make bulbs easy to care for, plant them in a blanket of groundcover. The groundcover covers up the bare spots left behind when the bulbs go dormant. Because the foliage of larger bulbs such as daffodils becomes unsightly as it yellows, you may have the chore of removing it in early summer. (Never remove green foliage, or you'll starve the bulbs and prevent them from reblooming.) Or, you can hide withering foliage by interplanting spring-flowering bulbs with summer-flowering perennials—each grows and flowers in the same spot but at different times. The perennials' foliage grows up and around the yellowing bulb leaves.

## Right Plant, Right Place

The real secret of successful easy-care landscaping is picking the right plants—ones that not only flourish with minimum attention, but also contribute aesthetically to your garden. Look for plants with the following characteristics:

### Well Adapted

A basic fact of gardening is that plants thrive under their preferred growing conditions and struggle under adverse ones. So it makes sense to choose only those plants that are adapted to the conditions you have in the various parts of your property.

If your water supply is limited, look for drought-tolerant plants. For a side yard shaded by the

---

# Undemanding Flowers for Easy-Care Gardens

This list of easy-care flowers includes annuals that don't need deadheading to promote blooming, long-blooming perennials that don't require staking or frequent division, and reliable bulbs that come back year after year. Your local nursery can tell you which flowers thrive in your climate and under your particular growing conditions.

**ANNUALS**
Cockscomb *(Celosia cristata)*
Cosmos *(Cosmos bipinnatus)*
Creeping zinnia *(Sanvitalia procumbens)*
Dahlberg daisy *(Dyssodia tenuiloba)*
Edging lobelia *(Lobelia erinus)*
Forget-me-not *(Myosotis sylvatica)*
Garden verbena *(Verbena x hybrida)*
Impatiens *(Impatiens wallerana)*
Madagascar periwinkle *(Catharanthus roseus)*
Marigold *(Tagetes,* triploid hybrids only)
Sapphireflower *(Browallia speciosa)*
Swan river daisy *(Brachycome iberidifolia)*
Sweet alyssum *(Lobularia maritima)*

Wax begonia *(Begonia semperflorens)*

**PERENNIALS**
Astilbe *(Astilbe x arendsii)*
Balloonflower *(Platycodon grandiflorus)*
Bleedingheart *(Dicentra spectabilis)*
Butterflyweed *(Asclepias tuberosa)*
Coneflower *(Rudbeckia fulgida)*
Coralbells *(Heuchera sanguinea)*
Daylily *(Hemerocallis* cultivars)
English lavender *(Lavandula angustifolia)*
Fernleaf yarrow *(Achillea filipendulina)*
Hosta *(Hosta* cultivars)
Oriental poppy *(Papaver orientale)*

Peony *(Paeonia lactiflora)*
Siberian iris *(Iris sibirica)*
Stokes/aster *(Stokesia laevis)*
Stonecrop *(Sedum spectabile)*
Threadleaf coreopsis *(Coreopsis verticillata)*

**BULBS**
Autumn crocus *(Colchicum autumnale)*
Crocus *(Crocus x vernus)*
Daffodil *(Narcissus* cultivars)
Grape hyacinth *(Muscari armeniacum)*
Siberian squill *(Scilla siberica)*
Snowdrop *(Galanthus nivalis)*
Spanish bluebell *(Endymion hispanicus)*
Summer snowflake *(Leucojum aestivum)*
Windflower *(Anemone blanda)*

*To get the most bang for your buck, choose trees and shrubs with more than one season of interest. For instance, beach rose (Rosa rugosa) bears gorgeous pink, rose-red, or white flowers in early summer, followed by showy red berries in fall.*

*One rule of easy-care gardening is to select plants that need no pruning or pest control. While most roses attract insects and fungal diseases and need careful pruning, this polyantha shrub rose ('The Fairy') blooms all summer long and remains pest-free without any attention from you.*

house next door, choose plants that thrive in low light. A damp spot is ideal for moisture-loving plants—they will be happy without your having to provide extra care. If a certain pest is serious in your area, choose plants that aren't bothered by it.

### Native and Non-Native Choices

Native plants—plants indigenous to your area of the country—are well adapted to your climate and particular growing conditions. By selecting the most beautiful native trees, shrubs, and wildflowers of your re-

gion, you can create a lovely easy-care landscape. The design can be naturalistic or more formal, but its ease of care comes from the well-adapted plants in it.

But remember, not all native plants are problem-free. Some are susceptible to insects and diseases, and all must be grown in their preferred growing conditions. Also, don't restrict yourself to native plants in the belief that they're always the best adapted. Well-adapted plants from other regions and countries can expand your options. What matters most is whether a plant is suited to your climate and particular growing conditions.

For example, plants from Chile, South Africa, Australia, New Zealand, and Mediterranean countries do well in coastal California, since all of these areas share mild winters and dry summers. Rhododendrons and azaleas from mountainous regions of Asia thrive in the cool, moist Pacific Northwest, which offers similar growing conditions to those found in Asia.

### Easy to Grow

Look for plants that grow well on their own without much attention from you. Often these plants are described as "tough," "rugged," "undemanding," or "easy care." Beware of such designations in plant catalogs from other regions, since a plant may not be easy to grow everywhere. A local nursery is a good source of

information about plants that do well in your area.

Don't reject some plants out of hand just because they're considered demanding—they may have related species and cultivars that are more carefree. For example, species roses and many modern shrub roses are much tougher and more disease-resistant than hybrid rosebushes. Plant breeders devote a great deal of effort to improving plants and making them easier to grow, so look for new choices on a regular basis.

### Resistant to Pests and Diseases

For a plant to be truly easy care, it must resist the pests and diseases that cause significant problems in your area. Battling bugs and blights is time consuming, and your efforts may be wasted in the end. Some damaging organisms can wipe out plantings overnight, leaving you with gaping holes in the landscape.

Talk to local nursery staff and to other people who garden in your area, and ask which pests pose problems locally. Find out which plants have withstood these troublesome pests, and put them among your top choices if they meet your needs in other respects. If you are thinking of growing plants that are especially vulnerable, cross them off your list.

### Matched to the Space

When you're considering plants for a particular spot in the landscape, choose those that won't outgrow

*The most attractive and easiest type of landscape to care for is a mixed border that combines trees, shrubs, and groundcovers with flowering perennials and annuals. The woody plants provide year-round structure and texture, as well as color. And because they are planted in small quantities, annuals and perennials don't require time-consuming care.*

Design: Conni Cross

their allotted space. Force a shrub into a tight spot, and it will need constant pruning over the years to keep it in bounds. But give it enough growing room, and it will develop its natural shape without impinging on structures or other plantings.

For tight spots, consider compact, dwarf, or slow-growing cultivars. By using these versions for foundation plantings, you can avoid the problem of plants growing up over the windows and into the eaves.

In general, you should take into account mature size when deciding placement in the garden. But with large trees, especially slow-growing ones that will probably outlive you, space according to the design size— usually the height it will reach in 15 to 20 years. Ask your nursery staff or tree supplier for advice about the amount of space you should allot such trees.

## Low-Maintenance Design ABCs

Landscape design professionals follow the same artistic principles in designing a low-maintenance yard as they do any other yard. They regard the space as an outdoor room, where they will create a floor, walls, and a ceiling by combining compatible plants and structures. But the experts don't stop there when de-

signing for easy care—and neither should you. Here are some of their professional techniques for making beautiful gardens that are easy to maintain:

### Mostly Mixed Borders

Low-maintenance landscapes often contain mixed borders consisting of a combination of shrubs, groundcovers, ornamental grasses, perennials, bulbs, annuals, and even small trees. Attractive woody plants give the border a permanent structure and year-round good looks. Herbaceous flowers add color, although too many of them can make a border look barren in late fall and winter.

A mixed border is suitable for both foundation plantings and property borders. It can be any size you like, from a fairly small entry area to the entire perimeter of the yard bordering the lawn. Just be sure it's big enough to include masses of plants—a border with just one of each shrub or perennial isn't nearly as effective. A mixed border should also be sufficiently large that a small tree won't overwhelm it. A gently curving shape looks best in informal gardens. Don't forget to plan stepping-stones or other access into the border at the widest areas.

The simplest way to build the border is to locate the woody plants first, then fill in with herbaceous plants. Begin with a small tree as a focal point. (You might want to put one in each of the widest sections of the border.) The tree should have some feature that makes it a good accent, such as an attractive branching pattern or colorful bark. Next, place groups of evergreen and deciduous shrubs underneath and to the sides and back of the tree. If you locate the border in front of a fence or wall, plant vines to grow over the structure.

Add groundcovers beneath the tree and shrubs, and put groups of perennials and low ornamental grasses in front of and between shrub groups. Bulbs should go in the groundcover beneath the deciduous shrubs and should be interplanted with the perennials. If you want to include annuals, intersperse them in large drifts among the perennials.

If you organize the space well, you should be able to pack your favorite plants into the border. A successful mixed border looks like a landscape in microcosm, yet it will be easily manageable because the space is limited and well planned.

*Shrubs that have golden, blue-gray, or bronze-red leaves create beautiful color contrasts and eye-catching focal points. And the color lasts for months— much longer than the fleeting show put on by flowers.*

## Year-Round Interest from Low-Maintenance Plants

A well-planned landscape offers appealing features throughout the year, rather than depending on spring and summer flowers for interest and looking ho-hum the rest of the time. Luckily, many features that make a garden interesting don't require high maintenance, so lazy gardeners have just as much opportunity as anyone else to turn out a landscape with year-round pizzazz.

Trees and shrubs are easier to care for than flowering perennials and annuals, and they can be just as colorful if you choose wisely. The ornamental berries and fruits produced by many flowering shrubs and trees provide welcome splashes of color in fall and winter, when the garden can look dreary.

Some species produce long-lasting fruit that ripens in summer or fall and hangs on well into winter. Various species of cotoneaster and pyracantha brighten the scene with red or orange berries. Most hollies bear red berries, although some types turn out bright yellow ones. Several species of beautyberry produce persistent lavender fruits. Snowberry is among the most reliable sources of tenacious white berries. Even the showy cones of some evergreen conifers, including many spruces and pines, add interest to the landscape.

Some plants dress up the scene with ornamental bark, which is especially stunning in winter. For example, the trunk and branches of 'Sango Kaku' Japanese maple are brilliant coral-red. Crape myrtle's gray or light brown outer bark flakes off to expose smooth pink inner bark. The mahogany bark of paperbark maple peels back in papery patches to reveal gleaming cinnamon brown beneath.

An easy-care landscape relies on many woody plants, which don't need much routine care, yet capture your interest throughout the seasons. For example, many types of viburnum bear showy flowers in spring, flaming foliage in fall, and bright red or black berries that last from fall into winter. Cornelian cherry starts its year-long show in late winter with clouds of small yellow blossoms on bare twigs, followed by handsome glossy green leaves and large edible scarlet fruit in summer, and then red fall foliage— not to mention the continuing display of its gray-and-tan mottled bark.

### Plan for a Succession of Bloom

Flower color is the most obvious feature of interest in any landscape. Most gardens tend to burst into spring bloom and then quickly turn uniformly green. Landscape professionals strive for some flower color during the entire growing season, planning for a succession of bloom from trees, shrubs, bulbs, and perennials. That way, flowering is staggered throughout the growing season instead of concentrated during a month or two in spring.

You can stretch out the blossoms further by choosing easy-care, long-blooming flowers. This is especially important in small gardens where every plant must pull its own weight. (See the list of long-blooming, easy-care perennials on page 15.)

***Rely on Colorful Foliage*** Most people associate colorful leaves with autumn. It's true that many deciduous trees and shrubs turn vibrant shades of red, orange, yellow, and purple in the fall in cold-winter areas, though the phenomenon is less common in mild climates. Certainly, you should plan for these eruptions of short-lived color, but for prolonged interest, try growing plants that bear colorful foliage throughout the growing season. You'll find plants with red, copper, purple, yellow, gray, and silver leaves. Even green leaves come in many gradations, from pale apple green and chartreuse through bright emerald to avocado and deep bottle green. Many needled evergreens bear gorgeous blue-gray or golden-hued leaves.

Use shrubs and trees with colorful foliage as focal points in the landscape. Colorful leaves endure much longer than blossoms and are an easy-care method of providing months of contrasting color to jazz up nearby greenery.

Some of the most attractive plants have variegated leaves that are marbled, spotted, or edged with white or yellow. The blue flowers of 'Burgundy Glow' bugleweed may come and go in spring, but its tricolored pink, burgundy-purple, and creamy-white leaves endure throughout the growing season.

*Plan for Long-Lasting Interest* Most easy-care gardeners want a lot of interest and diversity in the garden throughout the year without having to keep replanting. The trick is to choose plants that contribute something of interest in at least two seasons. The contribution may be a single feature that spans several seasons, such as colorful bark. Or it may be a progression of features, such as spring flowers followed by late-summer berries, or colorful fall foliage followed by a handsome branching pattern in winter.

Yet another way to create long-lasting interest is to choose plants that have intriguing silhouettes or shapes. Some of the most spectacular choices are deciduous plants whose outlines become most apparent in late fall and winter when the limbs are bare, such as ornamental weeping cherries and Kousa dogwood. In addition, some plants have contorted, gnarled branches. One of the best examples is a cultivar of European filbert called 'Harry Lauder's' walking stick.

Planning for enduring appeal is one of the most important aspects of easy-care landscaping, so make it a top priority when you select plants. Be demanding—ask a lot from the plants you choose. If the first plant you're considering doesn't measure up, go on to the next plant and see if it does.

**Use Large Areas of Hardscape**
Landscape professionals refer to all the nonplant surfaces in a garden—walkways, decks, patios, terraces, walls, fences, arbors, gazebos, benches, and so on—as hardscape. Although these inanimate features may require periodic sweeping or some other limited maintenance, they don't have to be routinely watered, fertilized, pruned, divided, or monitored for pests, as plants do. So the more hardscape in a yard, the less maintenance required.

Design professionals don't recommend blanketing your yard with hard surfaces at the expense of greenery and colorful flowers. Rather, they advise incorporating hardscape if it serves some purpose or contributes to the aesthetics of the landscape. For instance, you may want to replace a section of lawn that you *don't* use for recreation with an attractive flagstone terrace that you *will* use for seating.

## Plant Marriages

Having a yard full of plants, all with similar shapes—for example, rounded, vase-shaped, spiky, oval, weeping, pyramidal, columnar, or irregular—makes for a boring landscape, so vary the forms. Resist the impulse to use one of each form in a grouping, because that just makes a busy, cluttered mess. Instead, arrange plants with similar forms in masses, then group masses of two or three different forms together. Choose a single plant of another shape as an accent—a weeping or spiky plant serves well in this role.

Monotony of texture (how fine or coarse a plant looks) is just as boring as plants with all the same shape, so use a little variety here, too. Plants with small, delicate, smooth, or glossy foliage tend toward fine texture, while those with large, bold, rough, or dull foliage tend toward coarse texture. Boxwoods and azaleas are said to be fine-textured, while Japanese aralias and Southern magnolias are described as coarse.

Design: Conni Cross

*Consider plant size and shape when arranging shrubs. Here, three columnar evergreens are balanced by low-spreading and rounded shrubs to create an effective design. Although the evergreen plants do not bloom, their dark green, blue-gray, golden, and bronze leaves combine to create a colorful display.*

*One way to reduce maintenance on a large property is to design an oasis of high-care traditional plantings near the house and an easy-care, naturalistic planting on the rest of the property. Here, an easy-care landscape solution is achieved by placing the lawn near the house where the kids play, and a meadow of wildflowers at the property's perimeter.*

Those in between are characterized as medium-textured. Planting masses of fine-textured plants in front of gradually coarser ones creates a pleasing pattern.

### Group Compatible Plants

Upkeep is easier and more efficient when plants with similar growing requirements are grouped together. If several plants require more acid or alkaline conditions than your soil provides naturally, you'll find it easier to dig out a single bed and maintain the right conditions there than in scattered locations. In dry-summer climates, simplify irrigation by grouping plants with similar moisture needs.

Keep in mind that neighboring plants must also be compatible visually. Make sure their colors, shapes, leaf textures, and bloom times work together. What's the point of having an easy-care landscape if the plants grouped for efficiency's sake look terrible together?

### Efficient Interplanting

For some reason, many home gardeners are afraid to let different kinds of plants mingle and grow together. They plant bulbs in a bulb bed, flowering perennials in a perennial bed, and groundcovers in isolated patches. The bulbs produce lovely blossoms for a short period, then leave you with dying foliage and bare spots. The perennials, grown alone, can look lifeless until they begin to flower. The groundcover does its job of blanketing the soil, but it's not being used to full advantage.

The canny low-maintenance landscaper interplants bulbs and perennials with the groundcover. The result is a long season of color in the same location, plus camouflage for withered bulb foliage. An evergreen groundcover hides the absence of perennials that die back in winter, and serves as a counterpoint to late-winter and early-spring bulbs.

### Think Small and Efficient

Just because you've opted for low maintenance doesn't mean you can't enjoy some elements that demand more care and coddling, such as a water garden or flower beds. If you scale down the number of high-maintenance features, or the amount of space devoted to them, they won't be such a chore to keep up. For example, plant six instead of six dozen rosebushes; grow vegetables intensively in a few raised boxes instead of filling a half-acre; or plant a single row of easy-care berry bushes instead of a whole orchard of demanding fruit trees.

### An Oasis in Suburbia

Another way to scale down is with oasis landscaping. (See page 102.) Like a fertile, green island in the midst of a desert, the oasis landscape concentrates high-maintenance features in a small area and makes the rest of the yard low-maintenance.

Centuries ago, this type of landscape was commonplace in arid regions of the Mediterranean, where irrigation water was scarce. Gardeners devoted a walled courtyard or other limited space to moisture-loving plants. They used drought-tolerant plants in the remainder of the landscape—or even allowed the area to grow wild.

The oasis concept can be adapted to any region and to situations other than drought. This method of landscaping reduces overall maintenance while creating a lovely setting around your home. For instance, if you have a large property, don't plant several acres of lawn. Instead, create a traditional landscape of lawn with shrub and flower borders near your home, and leave the rest as a low-maintenance naturalistic meadow or woodland.

### Allow Growing Room

Nothing makes more work for the aspiring easy-care gardener than putting too many plants in too tight a space. Soon they'll outgrow the space and end up costing you time and money. Gardeners who make this mistake find themselves constantly cutting back to keep the plants in bounds and to uncover windows and walkways. Poorly placed shrubs create more work for you, since you must continually prune them to force them into their allotted space. (See page 42 for low-maintenance pruning methods.)

If you do nothing else, heed this basic tenet of low-maintenance landscaping: Give your plants adequate growing room. Take into account mature size when placing plants. If you're planting several shrubs, each of which reaches 4 feet wide at maturity, then space their trunks 4 feet apart. When they're fully grown, their branches will just touch. The planting may look sparse for the first year or two, but later on you'll be glad you spaced the shrubs correctly.

## Designing Easy-Care Lawns

Lawns are very demanding—they require regular mowing, edging, fertilizing, watering, weeding, thatching, aerating, raking, and, in many areas of the country, liming. Dealing with pests and diseases can be another time-consuming chore. Unfortunately, you can't procrastinate as much with a lawn as you can with other plantings, for turf can turn from gorgeous to ghastly very quickly.

Still, there are good reasons to have a lawn in areas where water isn't in chronic short supply. There's nothing like a lawn for kids' play or for setting off beds and borders, and no other groundcover withstands foot traffic as well.

But lawn care shouldn't feel like a life sentence without the possibility of parole. Instead of allowing a grassy patch of land to make unreasonable demands on your leisure time, use some of the following tactics to make the lawn more manageable:

### Reduce or Replace

You can reduce the drudgery of lawn care simply by reducing the size of the lawn. Don't use a lawn as a space filler: Put it where it serves

You can reduce yard and garden maintenance considerably by selecting plants that are well adapted to your climate and your property's growing conditions. Here, drought-tolerant native plants decorate an easy-care Texas garden.

Design: Conni Cross

Choose shrubs for foundation plantings that won't need constant pruning to keep them in bounds. Here, dwarf conifers and slow-growing, small-scale shrubs and trees create a welcoming entrance that's a breeze to care for.

your purpose, whether as a play surface or as a counterpoint to other plantings. In fact, plan the lawn first so that you incorporate only as much as you need and can easily maintain.

In areas where turf is unnecessary, install low-maintenance groundcovers and shrub or mixed borders instead. If you want to mimic the wide-open green expanse of a lawn, choose a ground-hugging plant such as bugleweed or wintercreeper. An-

other easy-care option is hardscape, including decks, patios, and gravel beds.

Meadows are often mentioned as alternatives to lawns, but don't be fooled into thinking that you can easily establish one just by sprinkling handfuls of wildflower seeds on the ground. (See page 9 for the correct way to install a meadow.)

If you have no use for a lawn on a small lot, then don't feel you have to include any turf at all. Some people think that even a small patch of grass is obligatory in a residential landscape. But why commit to lawn care if you don't need a lawn? Let others join the weekly mower brigade while you spend your time on more worthwhile activities.

## Avoid Slopes and Shade

Do yourself a favor and don't plant your lawn on a grade of 15 percent or more. Controlling a mower on

a steep incline provides a more challenging workout than most people want! Also water and fertilizer tend to run off slopes, resulting in a lawn with uneven color and dry spots.

The simplest, least expensive alternative to a lawn on slopes is to use deep-rooted, spreading groundcovers or shrubs that bind the soil and prevent erosion. Just be sure to dig out planting pockets so that water can soak in around the roots instead of running down the hill. Terracing is a more costly option, but it will create level planting areas.

Although some turf grasses tolerate low light, none do well in the deep shade found in heavily wooded areas, the immediate north side of a house, or narrow side yards next to tall buildings. The grass will fare poorly and may even die out. But unsuitable as these locations are for turf, they're perfect for shade-loving groundcovers, shrubs, and perennials.

*Without regular mowing—usually once or twice a week—lawn grass becomes unhealthy and unsightly. To reduce the time you spend on weekly garden chores, keep the lawn small and replace it with a deck or patio and mixed plantings.*

*A brick mowing strip provides an attractive way to keep a garden neat. The lawn mower wheels can move along the bricks for a close trim, and the bricks prevent grass from creeping into the bed and creating a weed problem.*

## Pick the Right Grass

Lawn grasses differ in terms of pest resistance, durability, water requirements, shade tolerance, and other characteristics. So if you're putting in a new lawn, be sure to choose one suited to your site. A well-adapted grass requires less work than one struggling under hostile conditions.

In many areas of the country, only a single choice will be suitable, and it will be the only one you'll find at nurseries. But in some regions, you'll have a choice of, say, Kentucky bluegrass or tall fescue, as well as a mix of several grasses. Your selection can determine how much mowing and watering you will have to do.

The Lawn Institute recommends the following grasses for low-maintenance lawns: Kentucky bluegrass cultivars with small amounts of perennial ryegrass and fine fescue for the Northeast and Midwest; 100-percent tall fescue for the transition zone between North and South; hybrid Bermuda grass for the South; buffalograss for arid regions of the Southwest; bluegrass for higher elevations of the Southwest; and Colonial bentgrass and fine fescue for the Pacific Northwest. In many

cases, there are improved cultivars of these grasses that outperform the standard species. Ask your local nursery or county agricultural extension agent for recommendations.

## Plan an Easy-to-Mow Shape

A lawn with a scalloped edge or one with tentacles stretching to various parts of the yard may look interesting, but it's a pain in the neck to mow. And an odd-shaped lawn is difficult to irrigate without wasting water.

The simplest layout for mowing or watering is a square or rectangle. Although these simple geometric shapes are fine for a formal landscape, they're not the most visually pleasing for an informal one—a free-form lawn has more appeal in a casual setting. Don't get too fancy with the edges, however. Keep in mind that a semicircle or other shape with gentle, broadly sweeping curves, rather than sharp bends, is easy to maneuver around with a mower and looks attractive, too. Gentle curves also allow for reasonably efficient spacing of irrigation heads.

## Install a Lawn Edging or Mowing Strip

Edgings or mowing strips between lawns and garden beds are indis-

pensable in most low-care landscapes because they prevent plants from escaping their boundaries. An effective edging keeps lawn grass from creeping into beds and borders, where it becomes a weed, and keeps groundcover plants out of the lawn. In addition, edgings give the lawn crisp lines that create a neat and tidy appearance with less work. Properly installed, an edging or mowing strip allows close mowing and does away with time-consuming trimming.

Of course, edgings are appropriate only when they fit your garden's style. They're out of place in most naturalistic gardens, since you don't find them in nature. If you want to use edgings in a highly naturalistic garden, you'll have to make them look natural, which can be difficult to do.

*Edging Choices* Landscape designers and architects often install steel edging used for driveway curbs as a lawn border. It's pliant enough for curves and looks inconspicuous. Steel edging is an expensive option, however, and many do-it-yourselfers use less costly types of borders made from vinyl or aluminum.

For best appearance and durability, use a dark brown vinyl edging

with a tough tubular top so that it can withstand occasional nicks from the mower blades. You can easily install this edging by digging a trench along the outlines of the lawn and burying the edging up to its tubular top. You can make the vinyl more flexible and easier to shape into curves by letting it sit in the sun before installation. Don't make the common mistake of installing the edging too high—the tubular edge should rest just above the soil surface. Properly installed, the edging is inconspicuous (the top should be hidden by the grass) and low enough that the mower blades will clear it as you guide the wheels to the other side of the edging.

*Mowing Strips*  Among the biggest time-savers is a ground-level mowing strip installed all the way around the lawn. Not only does it prevent grass from growing into adjoining beds and borders, it also gives the lawn a decorative border and crisp shape without your having to continually chop at the edges. Bricks, large flat stones, and poured concrete make effective, long-lasting mowing strips that can follow the outline of a free-form lawn. When set flush with the grass, they provide a stable base for mower wheels to ride on.

Set bricks flat on a bed of sand, with a weed barrier beneath to prevent weeds from pushing through. A row of bricks, set on end along the strip of flat bricks, extends deep enough into the soil to stop grass roots from tunneling under and becoming a weed problem in the planting border on the other side.

A mowing strip cannot restrain vining groundcovers from leaping across to the other side, but it makes trimming the groundcover back and keeping the lawn shape tidy an easy

*Weeds often pop up between paving stones and bricks in a walkway and are a nuisance to pull. You can crowd out weeds by planting paving plants, such as the Irish moss used here, between the pavers.*

chore. As you run the mower wheels along the strip, the blades trim back most of the invading vines, keeping them in place. Extra trimming may be required once or twice a year, but the mowing strip shows you exactly where to trim.

Some gardeners design taller edgings made from fieldstone, logs, or bricks set diagonally on end, but these prevent the mower from getting close enough to trim the lawn edge. These edgings require hand-trimming each time you mow—an extra chore that you probably don't want. Use these decorative tall borders only where there's no grass on either side.

## Avoid Obstacles

Any obstacles in your mowing path slow you down and prolong maintenance, so don't clutter the lawn with solitary plants or with objects such as birdbaths and garden ornaments. (Save these ornaments for beds and borders.) Walkways through the lawn are fine, as long as the edges are flush with the grass so the mower can go right over the top.

Remove low-hanging tree or shrub branches that block your way or make you stoop while mowing. Planting a lawn too close to a fence also makes mowing difficult—better to have a groundcover planting or shrub border in front of the fence.

*Constructed properly from quality materials, patios and decks are long-lasting, easy-care, permanent additions to your home's landscape. For a patio, be sure to use paving bricks, which are harder, thicker, and more durable than building bricks.*

Surface tree roots are another obstacle to mowing and lawn health, so ring trees with mulch or groundcovers.

*Group Plantings in Beds* Scattering trees and shrubs willy-nilly throughout the lawn isn't the most attractive way to position plants, and it makes more work when you're mowing. You have to negotiate your way carefully around each plant, stooping to avoid branches and limbs, unless you ring each tree or shrub with mulch or groundcovers; however, having so many circled plantings looks downright odd. You can simplify mowing and improve the looks of your landscape by grouping landscape plants in island beds or borders.

If you plan to locate planting beds within the lawn rather than at the perimeter, make them large and shape them so that mowing around them isn't a chore. You may want to place the beds fairly close together so that the lawn between them serves as a grassy pathway. The paths should be wide enough for you to easily steer the mower back and forth two or three times.

*Get Rid of Grass Under Trees* If possible, eliminate lawn under trees. With the lawn gone, you don't have to painstakingly maneuver the mower around the trunks to avoid nicking or bruising the bark, which can injure the trees, nor do you have to hand-trim the grass immediately next to the trunk and further risk damaging the tree. With grass gone, you don't have to worry about surface roots of shallow-rooted trees interfering with the lawn mower. And both the lawn and the tree grow better when they aren't competing with each other for water and nutrients.

Most trees used in the easy-care designs in this book are placed within mixed borders or beds of shade-tolerant groundcovers, which saves on maintenance. If a tree is situated alone in the lawn, a wide ring of mulch surrounds it. It's best to make the ring a little larger than the tree canopy. If the tree is very young, extend the ring to where you expect the canopy to be in several years, or expand it as the tree grows. If you decide on a groundcover, choose one for its ability to absorb litter from the tree.

## Designing to Keep Out Weeds

Getting rid of weeds is a tedious task that never really ends, since weeds have an annoying habit of popping up no matter what you do. But you can drastically reduce the number of weeds you must deal with by making it difficult for them to establish themselves in your landscape.

The most important thing to remember is that weeds love bare soil. Leave them an opening, and you can count on them showing up. But put plants, mulch, or hardscape there, and you don't give them much growing room.

Design garden beds and borders so that plants grow densely together, shading out weeds. Lay out the planting so that the leaves of adjacent plants will overlap slightly at maturity. Further deter weeds by growing groundcovers under the taller plants. Also, use groundcovers to blanket large expanses—they'll discourage weeds, just as a thick, healthy lawn does.

Mulching is another important way to prevent weeds, especially when your landscape is new and plantings haven't filled in yet.

## Guidelines for Designing an Easy-Care Landscape

Easy care doesn't mean sacrificing the grace, charm, liveliness, and color that make a landscape so pleasing. For a beautiful garden that doesn't hold you hostage, just follow these work-saving tips from the professionals:

- Choose disease-resistant, well-adapted plants that don't need constant pest proofing, watering, pruning, staking, or other pampering to thrive.

- Choose easy-care, long-lived perennials and flowering shrubs rather than high-maintenance annuals to provide floral beauty.

- Plant dwarf or slow-growing types of shrubs, which won't need routine pruning to keep them in bounds.

- Choose trees with compound leaves (leaves made up of two or more tiny leaflets) to make fall raking an easy chore.

- Underplant trees with groundcovers that absorb fallen leaves and debris, to reduce cleanup.

- Reduce the size of the lawn and replace the turf with groundcovers, hardscape, or mulched shrub borders.

- Keep to a minimum unconnected lawn areas and specimen plantings in the lawn to ease mowing chores.

- Install permanent borders or edgings between the lawn and planting beds to eliminate the need for weekly trimming of lawn edges and to keep grass out of shrub and flower beds.

- Install weed barriers beneath gravel, paving, or mulched paths to prevent weeds.

A thick layer of mulch robs weed seeds of the light they need to germinate, and slows down perennial weeds. Choose organic mulches (those made of once-living material, such as wood chips or pine needles) for planted areas, since they break down over time and improve the soil. Pile the mulch 4 to 6 inches high to deter weeds, and add more each year as it settles and decays. Take care not to pile mulch against plant stems, which can rot the plants.

Inorganic mulches (made of non-living material such as gravel) are better for pathways and other un-planted areas where you want the mulch to remain intact. (See page 40 for information on plastic and fabric weed barriers.)

Weeds will infiltrate patios and walkways made of bricks or flagstones set on sand or soil. You can stop the weeds by setting the bricks or stones on a bed of concrete and mortaring the joints. For a more casual look, plant small-scale groundcovers in the joints of unmortared stones—these will smother most weeds. Choose types that tolerate light foot traffic, such as creeping thyme or Irish moss.

## Planning for Minimum Cleanup

If you want an attractive landscape that doesn't need constant manicuring to maintain its appeal, think ahead during the design process. There are ways to reduce—sometimes drastically—the amount of time spent raking leaves, picking up fallen fruit, and performing other cleanup chores.

An authentic woodland is strewn with fallen leaves and twigs, so why should a re-created one be any different? No one removes withered leaves or seed stalks from a real meadow, so why should you tidy up yours? If you want to straighten up a little more than nature does, you can put in as little or as much work as you desire, since there are no rigid rules about how the landscape should look.

If you desire a more orderly yard, take a few simple measures to lessen cleanup. If you live in a region where deciduous trees and shrubs are predominant in landscapes, don't restrict yourself to them. Consider also using evergreens, which drop some leaves throughout the year rather than losing their foliage all at once.

## Modifying a High-Maintenance Yard

If you already have a basically pleasing landscape but find the upkeep too demanding, there's no need to rip everything out and start from scratch. Why sacrifice the time it took to get your landscape to maturity and wait for a new one to get established? Instead, you can modify it so that it needs less maintenance.

Begin by deciding which features you want to keep and which should be replaced. A good rule is to avoid removing more than you can replace immediately. It's better to install the landscape in stages rather than have large expanses of bare ground where weeds can take over.

Think carefully before eliminating any trees, since new ones can take a long time to grow to maturity. It may make more sense to retain some undesirable trees until the new specimens you plant are big enough to take their places. And if your complaint about a particular tree is that it's messy, consider underplanting it with shrubs or groundcovers that will hide the litter, rather than cutting it down.

Sometimes simply moving plants makes them less demanding. For example, a moisture-loving plant located at the perimeter of the yard, and inconveniently far from the water supply, won't be as much trouble when relocated closer to the house. Plants that need special handling demand less of your time if they're clustered rather than scattered throughout the yard.

If you're spending more time than you want to on lawn care, consider the many ways to lessen the workload. You can reduce the amount of turf, or even replace it with groundcovers, if you have no use for a lawn. If the shape of the lawn makes it laborious to mow and you spend half your time edging the grass, then redesign the lawn and put in a mowing strip. If trees slow down the mowing, then remove grass from underneath the canopies and ring the trees with mulch or groundcovers.

Tending large flower beds and borders can be arduous, especially if you're growing high-maintenance annuals. If this is a problem, reduce the size of the plots and put in easy-care perennials. Small beds and borders can be extremely effective if they are in scale with their surroundings. Another option—and one requiring even less maintenance—is a mixed planting (see Mixed Borders on page 17), which contains many permanent plants and a year-round structure.

Are you grappling with the time-consuming task of maintaining shrubs sheared into boxy shapes? There's no need for you to be locked into a formal landscape—it is possible to reclaim formally pruned shrubs. You can give them more natural shapes by changing your pruning practices. (See page 42.) The transformation may take several years, but it can be done.

Even a formal hedge can be modified. After all, a hedge is just a lot of shrubs planted close together. Dig up the plants, untangle them, and replant them farther apart for an informal hedge or screen. The key is to give them enough room to take on their natural shape.

Homeowners often shear shrubs to control their size. This is particularly true of foundation plants that were chosen without regard to how big they would eventually grow. Either drastically thin these overgrown plants, or replace them with lower-growing shrubs that won't need pruning. Thinning other overgrown shrubs in the landscape may help save them as well.

A beautiful landscape can be yours without having to spend a great deal of time taking care of it. It all starts with the planning and designs. Study the easy-care landscape plans in Chapters 3 and 4 to see how attractive they are, and observe the time-saving design ideas incorporated in them. You'll notice that trees and shrubs, grouped in borders and underplanted with groundcovers, form the backbone of most of the designs. Lawns are a manageable size, even on large properties, or are even eliminated in some cases. But the landscapes don't lack colorful flowers or foliage. On the contrary, they are brimming with an

Design: Conni Cross

*This clever landscape solution transformed useless space at the side of the house into an attractive, easy-care outdoor living space. A flagstone walk and patio replace the lawn, while slow-growing evergreens and flowering shrubs provide structure and texture.*

ever-changing display of attractive plants. It's easy to have a gorgeous low-maintenance landscape when you know how.

At least one of the 41 professionally designed landscape plans in this book is bound to be suitable for your property. If you want to follow it exactly, you can order a large, detailed blueprint with a regionalized plant list. (See pages 154-157.) If it's not quite right as is, you can modify it to accommodate your needs or use it as a springboard for your own ideas. (See pages 136-145 to find out how to modify a plan.)

# CHAPTER 2

# Time-Saving Techniques and Tools

## *How to Make Efficient Use of the Time You Spend Yard Maintenance*

Design: Ireland-Gannon Associates

Being an easy-care gardener doesn't mean doing a slapdash job of maintenance or letting the landscape go to ruin. Rather, it entails using labor-saving techniques and tools to get through maintenance chores faster and more efficiently, leaving you with newfound time for more interesting activities.

If you've ever noticed one neighbor struggling with yard work while another polishes off the same tasks swiftly, you know there's an easy way and a difficult way to do almost anything. In this chapter, you'll read about many of the techniques and tools designed to simplify and speed up the major maintenance chores involved in caring for your landscape. You'll find out the easiest ways to mulch, plant, prune, fertilize, water, weed, mow, and clean up.

Each task is addressed in a separate section. You'll find tips on how to lighten your workload and spend less time on maintenance—for example, using a timer to turn the watering system on and off; mulching to discourage weeds; thinning shrubs instead of shearing them to promote slower, healthier growth; using an efficient mowing pattern to save steps; and leaving grass clippings on the lawn to save cleanup time and effort.

You'll also find descriptions of various tools to help you perform maintenance chores efficiently. Anyone who has wrestled with a poor tool and then switched to a better one knows what a difference the right implement can make! An undersized, rickety wheelbarrow easily tips over, while a large, well-built one is a pleasure to maneuver, even when fully loaded. Dull pruners tire your hand and mangle stems, while sharp ones make quick, easy cuts.

### Rules for Tools

You'll need specialized tools for digging, cutting, watering, hauling, and all the other tasks required for even a low-maintenance landscape. It's impossible to overemphasize the importance of having the right tool for the job, using it correctly, taking care of it, and storing it properly. An unsuitable or defective tool only prolongs the job and frustrates you.

*Shrubs, perennials, and groundcovers replace the lawn on this difficult-to-mow slope, while a large deck further reduces maintenance and provides a wonderful outdoor living space.*

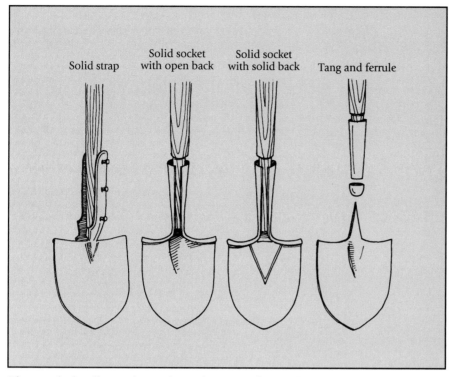

Solid strap | Solid socket with open back | Solid socket with solid back | Tang and ferrule

*The way the handle attaches to the working part of a tool determines the tool's strength and durability. The strongest attachment is a solid strap, where the blade and strap that extend up the handle are forged from one piece of metal. Solid-socket construction is less sturdy, but still quite strong. (Those with a solid, rather than open, back are stronger.) The least durable tools have a tang-and-ferrule construction, where a tang from the blade is inserted into the handle and covered with a ferrule; such a connection breaks easily when stressed.*

## Choosing Tools

Every nursery, garden center, hardware store, and home improvement outlet contains a tempting array of gardening tools designed for every conceivable task. Unless you plan your tool purchases carefully, you could end up with a lot of unnecessary gadgets or with tools that don't do the job properly. Consider these points when obtaining tools:

- Get only the tools you need and for which you have adequate storage space. Buy tools you will use regularly, and rent or borrow ones that you will rarely use.
- Most manufacturers make several grades of tools. Shop around to compare grades and manufacturers before making a major purchase. If you're unsure, rent or borrow the same model before buying it.
- Quality tools are the best bargains in the long run because they last longest, so purchase the best you can afford.

- Don't assume that power will necessarily simplify your life. Sometimes manual tools do a faster and more efficient job than ones powered by gas or electricity. Consider whether you can handle the noise, heft, or potential hazards of power equipment before deciding in its favor.
- When weighing gas versus electric, remember that gas-powered tools are more powerful than electric versions, but are also noisier. Electric tools have power cords that can tangle and may limit where you can use them.
- When purchasing tools that will get a lot of wear and tear, consider models made for contractors. They're usually sturdier than those marketed to homeowners.
- Pay close attention to tool construction, especially the way a handle attaches to the working end—the attachment largely determines the tool's

strength. The strongest—and the most expensive—have a solid socket or solid strap forged as a single piece with the tool's working end. Tang-and-ferrule construction is less sturdy.

- The best steel is labeled "tempered" or "heat treated" and should be "forged" rather than stamped out of sheet metal. Stainless steel tools are ideal, since they won't rust, but they're very expensive.
- Wooden handles should be free of knots and imperfections. The material of choice is ash; hickory runs a close second.
- Choose the handle length that matches your height. Long handles on digging tools provide more leverage and require less stooping, while short handles are less cumbersome in tight spots.

## Less Work Planting

Gardeners with sandy or loamy soil that's naturally easy to dig may not appreciate the frustration of gardeners who must dig in hard, clayey soil. Just digging a few small holes in unyielding terrain can wear you out and spoil your enthusiasm for landscaping.

The best way to improve the workability of hard soil and make planting easier is to add an organic soil amendment, such as well-rotted manure or compost. If you improve an entire planting area all at once, then future planting is much easier and plants grow better. Lay about 2 to 4 inches of organic material, such as compost or rotted manure, on top of the soil, then incorporate it as deeply as you can by turning it into the soil with a garden fork. For large areas, it pays to rent a power tiller with long tines or to hire someone to do the heavy labor for you.

Even if you don't amend the soil (and you may not want to when planting native plants), you can dig more easily if the soil is a little moist, rather than dry or sopping wet. Either water the soil thoroughly the day before planting and let it dry out just enough so it's crumbly, or dig a few days after a good rain.

Observing the following planting tips helps you conserve time and effort:

- It's faster to excavate a shallow bed for a mass of bulbs than to plant them in individual holes—and they'll look better, too!
- When planting balled-and-burlapped (B&B) shrubs, remove the burlap only from the top of the plant; what remains underground will rot away. (Remove all plastic netting, or plastic "burlap," however.)
- Make holes for B&B and container plants only as deep as the rootball and about twice the diameter—making holes bigger is a waste of time.
- Planting during the relative cool of the morning or evening, or during overcast or misty days is easier on both you and the plants.

## Planting Tools

Planting goes much faster when you use the right implements. Here's an overview of common planting tools intended for digging holes, turning the soil, and smoothing the soil:

*Shovels* Although shovels are designed primarily for scooping and lifting soil and other heavy materials, American gardeners like to dig with them. The most common garden shovel has a pointy-tipped, rounded blade attached at a fairly acute angle to a long, straight handle. It's this angle that provides the leverage for scooping. For durability, get a shovel with a blade and shank forged from a single piece of steel. The strongest and most expensive types have a closed back—a metal triangle welded over the fold at the blade's back. It's important that the shovel's weight and the handle's length suit you, or you'll wear yourself out lifting heavy loads.

*Spades* The digging tool of choice among English gardeners is the garden spade, which has a flat rectangular blade connected at a slight angle to a short handle, usually ending in a D-shaped grip. The angle of attachment makes the spade ideal for digging straight-sided holes.

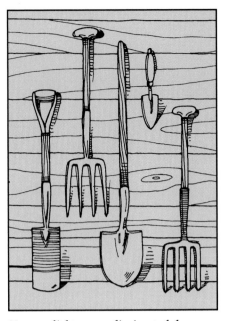

*You can lighten any digging task by selecting the right tool for the job at hand. Tools from left to right are:* **Spade:** *The flat, blunt blade and relatively short handle make it good for digging holes in planted areas;* **Spading fork:** *The rectangular, slightly curved tines and short handle make it an all-purpose fork for digging, turning, and mixing soil;* **Shovel:** *The pointed blade and long handle make it useful for digging large holes;* **Trowel:** *The short handle and various blade shapes work well for digging holes for bulbs, annuals, and other small plants;* **Garden fork:** *The straight square tines can be pushed deep into compacted soil to loosen and aerate it.*

A tread or footrest is desirable for extra leverage and to save wear and tear on your foot as you press down. The best spades are made of heavy-gauge steel with a solid-socket or solid-strap design—and they're typically made in England. For maximum leverage, the D-grip should come just below your waist when the blade is in the soil.

*Forks* These implements are handy for loosening or turning over the soil when you're preparing a planting bed or vegetable garden, as well as for turning compost and digging up plants. A fork is lighter than a shovel or spade, so is less tiring to use. The many types of forks vary in the number and shape of tines and in handle type.

For working the soil, you'll want a spading or garden fork with rectangular or square tines and a fairly

short, D-shaped handle for leverage. A pitchfork with curving, widely spaced, flat tines and a long, straight handle is useful for lifting lightweight materials. Pitchforks make lighter work of turning compost piles or moving heaps of debris. The sturdiest forks are made from tempered steel and are of solid-socket construction. Test the tines by pressing them together—they should spring back.

*Garden Rakes* These implements, which have short, rigid tines and long handles, are used to clear and smooth the soil. There are two types of garden rakes: level-headed and bow. On the level-headed type, a flat rod across the tines is attached directly to the handle, making it suitable for smoothing soil when it is flipped over. The lighter and springier bow rake, with an arch above the tines, is useful for cultivating, but less practical for leveling.

*Trowels* These versatile hand tools—with a metal scoop and a wooden, plastic, or metal handle—are used for digging shallow holes and prying up weeds. Trowels come with blades in various widths; wide-bladed models are multipurpose, while narrow types are useful for transplanting small seedlings and planting tiny bulbs. Pick a trowel that is easy to grip and feels comfortable in your hand. (You may want several types.) Keep in mind that those with brightly colored handles are less likely to get lost.

*Power Tillers* These gas-powered machines have tines that churn up the soil and turn it over. Usually the longer the tines, the larger and more expensive the tiller. This type of equipment might appeal to a gardener who regularly tills soil amend-

*Mulch applied thickly under shrubs, trees, and flowers reduces the time spent on gardening chores by preventing weeds and keeping the soil moist and cool. It also beautifies the landscape.*

ments into a big vegetable bed or annual flower plots. But easy-care gardeners who rely on permanent plants won't have much use for a power tiller, except during the initial stages of landscaping. If you decide you need one, renting is the most economical course. Be sure to use a tiller big enough to do the job efficiently.

## The Mechanics of Mulching

Mulching—spreading a protective layer of material on the soil beneath plants—is probably the single most important maintenance-saving procedure you can follow in your garden. A mulched garden is a healthier garden. The effort you spend laying down mulch each year will be paid back manyfold later in the year in terms of time saved on weeding, watering, and fertilizing.

Mulch prevents most weed seeds from germinating by depriving them of light, and any weeds that do grow

are easy to pull. In summer, mulch keeps the soil cool and moist, thus reducing the need for watering. In winter, mulch shields the soil from a cycle of alternate freezing and thawing, which can heave shallow-rooted plants right out of the ground. A layer of mulch also keeps soil, and soilborne disease organisms, from splashing on flowers and foliage during rain or irrigation.

Organic mulches—made from materials that once were alive, such as shredded bark, pine needles, chopped leaves, compost, and straw—are recommended for planted areas, since they gradually break down and filter into the soil. As the mulch slowly decomposes, it releases nutrients, which become available to plants. Mulch also encourages earthworm activity, which makes the soil more workable and further increases its nutrient content.

For an organic mulch to effectively control weeds, it should be

placed on soil that has been cleared of weeds. Pile on the mulch thick enough to discourage weed seeds from germinating, and add more each year as the layer shrinks. Chopped leaves break down rapidly, so start with a fairly thick layer—as much as 6 to 8 inches deep. A layer of wood chips can start off half as high, since they decompose more slowly. Once settled, the mulch shouldn't be thicker than about 4 inches, or it may smother plant roots.

Inorganic mulches—made from materials that were never alive, such as crushed rock or gravel—are generally better suited to unplanted areas in most gardens and climates, since they don't improve the soil. However, you'll probably want to use stones as a mulch around plantings in a rock garden or desert landscape. Rock looks more natural in these settings than wood chips or other organic materials.

Layer stones sparsely around plants so you don't smother the plant roots. In unplanted areas, such as gravel walks and patios, a layer of stones can be thin if applied over weed barrier cloth (see page 40), which prevents the stones from working themselves into the soil and "disappearing."

## Making Mulch

You can make your own mulch from yard refuse, such as fallen leaves or tree prunings. Use the leaves whole, or chop them with a power mower or special leaf shredder; grind prunings with a chipper/shredder. (See page 47 for more about these tools.) Some communities cut and chop prunings for homeowners as part of a waste recycling program. Tree-care companies are another source for quantities of wood chips—the chips are usually free or available for a small charge.

Mulches are available in bags at most garden centers and by the truckload at soil yards. The most economical choices are usually by-products of local crops or industries. Bark chips and shredded bark are least expensive where trees are harvested—for example, pine bark in the Northeast, and redwood and fir barks on the West Coast. Ground corncobs are among the choices in the Midwest, and peanut hulls are an option in the South.

Although mulch is considered indispensable, it can cause problems if used incorrectly. Keep the following in mind when mulching:

- Any mulches consisting largely of woody or dried vegetation temporarily deplete the soil of nitrogen as they decay. Before applying the mulch, apply a high-nitrogen fertilizer to offset the effect.
- Since a layer of mulch can slow soil warming, you may want to pull the mulch away from perennials and bulbs early in the year to speed plant growth.
- A wet mulch piled against tender stems of flowers and vegetables can cause the plants to rot. Keep the mulch about an inch away from stems.
- Mulch piled against woody stems of shrubs and trees can cause them to rot, and encourages rodents, such as voles and mice, to nest. Keep deep mulch 6 to 12 inches from tree trunks.
- In damp climates, organic mulches can harbor slugs and snails, which eat nearby plants. Avoid mulching near susceptible plants.
- Most organic mulch made from composted yard waste has a neutral pH—it's neither acidic nor alkaline. But if you're using acidic materials such as chopped oak leaves to mulch around plants that need neutral or slightly alkaline soil, mix in some lime beneath those plants.

## Less Work Fertilizing

Providing a supply of nutrients to the plants in your landscape keeps them healthy, but you want to tackle the task efficiently and avoid wasting time and money using unnecessary fertilizers. Many home gardeners waste time and money by routinely feeding all their plants, including trees and shrubs, which usually don't require any extra nutrients beyond what the soil supplies. Refraining from fertilizing these plants is doubly important for a low-maintenance gardener—you're not just eliminating a needless task, you're saving yourself the trouble of later pruning the excessive growth caused by over-fertilizing.

Another important work-saving step is to use organic mulches in shrub beds and borders, in perennial gardens, and under trees. The mulch slowly decomposes, filtering into the soil and providing nutrients to plants. Consequently, mulched plants don't need as much additional fertilizer as plants that don't have access to this nutritional source.

### Fertilizer Facts

The myriad of packaged fertilizers available nowadays varies in terms of nutrient content, forms of application, and the speed with which they release nutrients to plants. Once you understand a few simple facts about fertilizers, you can choose products intelligently without having to rely on advertising to help you decide.

*Organic mulches decay slowly and turn into humus, which improves the soil's texture, nutrient content, and water-holding capacity. Every spring after cleaning up the garden, apply fresh mulch on top of the old mulch to replace any that has decayed.*

Plants need fairly large amounts of the three major nutrients—nitrogen, phosphorus, and potassium—and smaller quantities of several minor nutrients. The three numbers on the front of a fertilizer package tell you the percentages, by weight, of the major nutrients. For example, the numbers 12-5-8 mean that the fertilizer contains 12 percent nitrogen, 5 percent phosphorus, and 8 percent potassium; the remainder is filler. If the fertilizer lacks a major nutrient, a zero appears in the sequence. For example, 0-10-10 contains no nitrogen and 10 percent each of phosphorus and potassium.

Nitrogen is the main nutrient you have to consider when buying a fertilizer, since it's the one nutrient in chronic short supply in all soils. But you don't want to add too much nitrogen, since it stimulates leafy growth—and excessive growth is weak and insect-prone, and also means more pruning. For general use, choose a balanced, all-purpose fertilizer containing

roughly equal amounts of the major nutrients, such as a 10-10-10 fertilizer. To encourage flowering or fruiting, use a low-nitrogen high-phosphorous fertilizer, such as 5-10-10 or 5-10-5.

Most fertilizers are either liquid or water soluble. Plants take up the nutrients in these fertilizers rapidly, showing a quick response. However, the effect of liquid plant foods is short-lived, and the nutrients must be replenished regularly. Liquid fertilizer that is not immediately taken up by plants leaches through the soil and can contaminate groundwater.

A smaller group of products, known as slow-release fertilizers, come in a dry form that won't dissolve in water. Available in granules, spikes, and pellets, these fertilizers break down slowly, gradually releasing nutrients to plants. Although more expensive than soluble fertilizers, slow-release fertilizers are a real time saver—they don't have to be applied nearly as often and are usually the best choice for plant health.

Organic materials such as manure and compost also slowly release nutrients as they decompose. You can use them to feed plants, although they may not be sold as fertilizer. Commercial fertilizers must have a consistent, verifiable nutrient content, so manure and compost, whose nutrient content varies, are marketed as soil amendments rather than fertilizers.

Some fertilizers are multipurpose. For example, various lawn fertilizers contain a weed killer or fungicide. Applying a multipurpose product saves time if your lawn happens to have a weed or fungus problem—but don't use it unless there is a problem. *Never* apply pesticides unnecessarily.

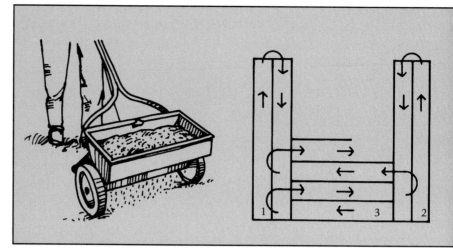

*A drop spreader applies lawn fertilizer (and weed killer and pesticides) without the danger of throwing chemicals into beds and borders where you don't want them. For most accurate coverage, apply the fertilizer at opposite ends of the lawn first (steps 1 and 2), being sure to overlap wheel tracks and shut off the spreader when turning. Next, run the spreader at right angles back and forth across the lawn, shutting off its flow as you turn (step 3).*

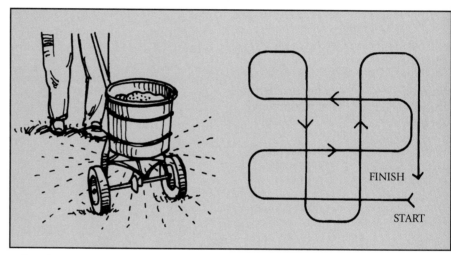

*A broadcast or whirlybird spreader throws out lawn chemicals in a wide arc. It is less accurate than a drop spreader, though it takes less steps to cover the same area. For the best coverage, follow the pattern shown here. Be sure to avoid getting weed killers on beds and borders, which could kill your valuable landscape plants.*

### Applying Fertilizer

Applying slow-release products by hand in small areas doesn't require a lot of effort, since you do it only occasionally. However, you'll want to speed up the fertilizing process when you have to apply products more often or in larger areas, such as lawns. Here's an overview of some of the handier implements used for fertilizing:

*Lawn Spreaders* These devices have a hopper to hold dry material, and holes or slots through which to dispense it. They're used to apply granular fertilizers—as well as other dry substances such as lime, seeds, and weed killers—to lawns. There are two types of spreaders: broadcast (also called rotary) and drop. A broadcast spreader throws the material in a wide arc. You'll need a wheeled push model if your lawn is large, but a small handheld model operated by turning a crank is adequate for a small space. A wheeled drop spreader deposits the material through slots on the bottom. Drop models are more accurate than broadcast types, thus making them safer for applying weed killers. However, it takes longer to do the job, and you have to walk farther with

## How Much Water Does Your Lawn Really Need?

Most irrigated lawns are overwatered, which not only wastes water but is bad for the lawn's health. The amount of water a lawn needs varies according to climate and weather patterns. It's usually better to apply water deeply once or twice a week than to water shallowly more often. That way, grass roots are encouraged to grow down in search of water, and the lawn becomes healthier and more drought-tolerant. The following guidelines should help you to determine the right amount of water from combined rainfall and irrigation:

| CLIMATE | AVERAGE HIGH TEMPERATURE (F°) | WEEKLY WATER IN INCHES | WEEKLY WATER IN GALLONS PER 100 sq.ft. |
|---|---|---|---|
| Cool, humid | Under 70 | .70 | 43.4 |
| Cool, dry | Under 70 | 1.05 | 65.1 |
| Moderate, humid | 70-80 | 1.40 | 86.8 |
| Moderate, dry | 70-80 | 1.75 | 108.5 |
| Warm, humid | 80-100 | 2.10 | 130.2 |
| Warm, dry | 80-100 | 2.45 | 151.9 |
| Hot, humid | Over 100 | 2.80 | 173.6 |
| Hot, dry | Over 100 | 3.15 | 195.3 |

a drop spreader than with a rotary spreader.

It's a good idea to purchase a brand-name spreader, because fertilizer companies usually recommend spreader settings by brand name. With a generic spreader, you may have to estimate the setting and thus risk applying too much or too little fertilizer or weed killer.

*Hose-End Sprayers* These offer a fast, easy way to apply water-soluble fertilizers on lawns and other large plantings. They're also recommended for foliar spraying of shrubs and trees—you spray the fertilizer directly on the leaves, usually to correct some nutrient deficiency.

To operate a hose-end sprayer, fill the plastic container with the fertilizer concentrate and attach the device to the end of a hose. When you turn on the faucet, water enters the container, dilutes the fertilizer, and sprays it through a nozzle. The various sprayer models differ in dilution ratios, so look for one with easy-to-understand instructions. Also, make sure the spray pattern suits your needs.

*Fertilizer Injectors* One of these devices is attached to the main assembly of a drip irrigation system (see page 39) and dispenses diluted fertilizer automatically as the system waters the plants. You can keep the

canister filled so that it feeds plants every time you irrigate, or you can fill it periodically when you decide to fertilize. Check with your local building department before putting in a fertilizer injector—some communities require professional installation of a double-check valve to prevent fertilizer from accidentally being siphoned into the house water supply.

### Less Work Watering

Unless your landscape consists solely of drought-tolerant or native plants that need no supplemental moisture once they're established, you'll have to do some watering during the year. Since few climates—even rainy-summer regions—provide consistent moisture on a weekly basis, providing the balance is up to the gardener.

Grouping plants by moisture requirements simplifies irrigation—you can water one planting and leave the others alone, rather than watering some plants unnecessarily. This "zoning" is especially important in arid regions, where gardeners are responsible for supplying needed moisture throughout most of the year.

Regardless of where you live, be sure to place any plant that needs regular hand-watering within easy access of the water supply. Watering

becomes a real chore if you're forced to drag hoses or lug watering cans long distances.

The key to efficient irrigation is to water plants *only* when they need it, rather than on a set schedule that doesn't take rainfall, temperature, or plant preferences into account. Some plants require moister conditions than others, so you have to know the plants' needs. You can tell if it's time to water by sticking your finger into the soil in a plant's root zone. The soil should dry out completely between waterings for plants that like it dry, and never dry out completely for those that need moister conditions.

You can lengthen the interval between needed waterings, and thus save time and money in any climate, by improving your soil's water-holding capacity. Do this by digging in lots of decomposed organic matter before planting, then applying a thick layer of mulch to conserve soil moisture. Keeping weeds out is also important, since they consume water intended for desirable plants.

To take the guesswork out of lawn watering, many water companies—especially those in the West—offer their customers lawn-watering schedules based on local climatic conditions. When watering any planting, including a lawn, apply enough water to penetrate about 18 inches deep—wetting only the soil surface promotes shallow rooting and a greater reliance on water.

Even if your soil is moisture retentive, your plantings well organized, and your watering schedule efficient, irrigation is still a time-consuming chore. In many climates, the best way to save time and effort is to automate watering. The type of automation can be as simple as

a portable sprinkler hooked to a timer, or as sophisticated as a built-in system of drip lines or lawn sprinklers programmed to run on its own. (See below.)

The following is an overview of the gadgets, tools, and irrigation systems that can help simplify the task of watering:

## Garden Hoses and Attachments

Dealing with a hose that twists and cuts water to a dribble is a real nuisance, so choose a flexible type with a woven or belted interior surface that resists kinking. A rubber hose is more durable and weather resistant than one made of nylon, vinyl, or a combination of vinyl and rubber. Since leaks often occur at fittings, a hose with brass fittings rather than plastic ones is a wise choice. Because it's easier to pull and store a short hose than a long one, choose a 25- or 35-foot-long hose. When you occasionally need a longer length, you can easily connect two or more short hoses together.

Garden hoses come in ½-, ⅝-, and ¾-inch diameters. You'll get more water faster with the largest-diameter hose, but hoses with wider diameters weigh much more and are more difficult to lug around than narrower ones. They also may deliver water faster than your soil can absorb it. If water is applied too fast, the excess runs off and is wasted.

Leave the shut-off valve on the nozzle open when the hose isn't in use—otherwise, water trapped inside expands in the heat and can burst the hose. Bring hoses indoors during winter in cold-winter regions to prevent water from freezing inside the tubing.

*Quick Couplers and Y-Connectors* Instead of having to screw attachments on and off garden hoses, quick couplers allow you to easily click the

*Dragging around long, heavy hoses that can twist and kink adds to the frustration of yard maintenance. The quick-release hose connector shown here helps make watering easier, because you can use shorter lengths of hose and attach and detach them easily.*

pieces together and snap them apart. For maximum convenience, keep a quick coupler on the end of each faucet and at the end of each hose, nozzle, and portable sprinkler. Brass couplers are more durable than plastic ones. To avoid trips to the faucet to turn the water off when you remove accessories, choose couplers with built-in valves so you can shut off the water flow.

Attach a handy little Y-shaped device to a faucet, and you'll get twice the utility from that faucet. Each arm of the Y has a shut-off valve so you can operate it independently. For example, you can connect a hose to each branch of the Y or divide a drip irrigation system into two sections. Metal connectors are much stronger than plastic ones.

*Porous Hoses* These are rubber hoses with tiny holes along their entire surface, allowing water to seep out slowly. These soaker hoses come in various lengths, from 25 to 500 feet. You can keep a porous hose permanently in a planting, buried by shallow mulch, and attach your regular garden hose to it when you need to water. The end cap should be removable so that you can flush the hose at least once a year. Porous hoses are often considered a com-

ponent of drip irrigation systems. (For more about drip technology, see page 39.)

## Portable Sprinklers

Portable sprinklers are most useful if you need to water a lawn or other large plantings only occasionally. A quality sprinkler emits water through brass fittings rather than through holes punched in the plastic or metal. Here are the basic types of portable sprinklers:

*Oscillating Sprinklers* These sprinklers have an arm that shoots water back and forth in a high arc. Because they propel water so high, oscillating sprinklers aren't suitable near trees or tall shrubs that could block the spray. The best models have gears that prevent overwatering at the end of the arc as the sprinkler changes direction.

*Rotary Sprinklers* These sprinklers have spinning arms that disperse water in a circle or square. Because they don't throw water as far as other portable sprinklers, they are suitable for small areas.

*Traveling Sprinklers* These are a type of rotary sprinkler that is propelled along as water is emitted. Lay out a hose in the pattern you want, and the sprinkler follows its path. A traveling sprinkler is costly but is more convenient than stationary types, which have to be moved.

*Impulse Sprinklers* These sprinklers send out powerful pulses of water in a large arc. The nozzle launches a stream of water, which a spring-loaded arm breaks into droplets as it moves through the arc. This type of sprinkler is suitable only for very large areas where the spray won't be blocked by shrubs or tree branches.

## Underground Sprinkler Systems

A permanent, automated in-ground sprinkler system is the easiest way to keep a lawn green. This type of system saves you from having to drag the hose and sprinkler from one part of the lawn to another—a seemingly endless summer chore in many areas of the country. Automated watering systems don't have to be limited to the lawn—they can be set up to care for beds and borders, too.

For such a system to be effective, the sprinklers must be positioned so

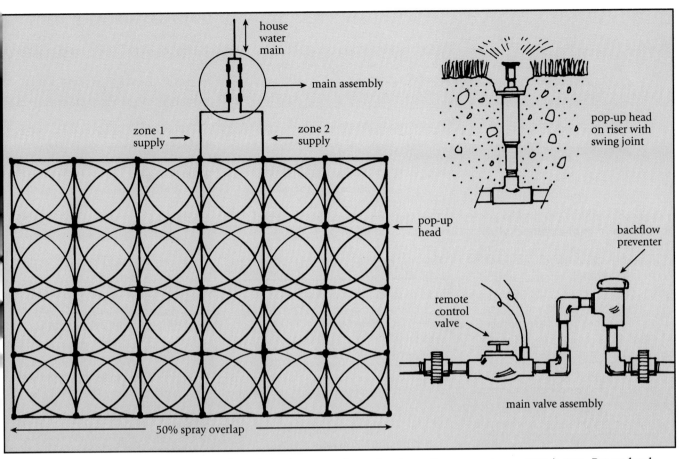

house water main

main assembly

zone 1 supply

zone 2 supply

pop-up head on riser with swing joint

pop-up head

backflow preventer

remote control valve

main valve assembly

50% spray overlap

*Lay out the sprinkler heads for an automatic lawn irrigation system in overlapping patterns, so water coverage is even. Pop-up heads can be adjusted to cover a full, three-quarter, half, or quarter circle.*

they distribute water uniformly in broadly overlapping sprays and deliver the proper amount of water to each of the various plantings in a landscape. Unfortunately, many sprinkler installers do not understand the water needs of plants and tend to set up a system so that all plants in the landscape get the same amount of water. Often that means too much water, and overwatering can kill plants. Each garden area should be separated into individual zones and watered according to each zone's needs. Any sprinkler installer who tells you otherwise is uninformed and therefore untrustworthy.

A system should be divided into sections or zones, each operated by its own valve, so that the water dispersed by any single section won't exceed the capacity of the home's water supply. When connected to an automatic timer or controller (see page 38), each section can be programmed to deliver water at certain times on certain days for a specified length of time. That way, lawns,

which need more water than established trees and shrubs, can be watered more often than foundation plantings or shady flower beds.

### Do-It-Yourself Sprinkler Installation

The basic underground sprinkler system hasn't changed much over the years, except that now PVC is almost exclusively used for the underground piping, making systems easier to install for do-it-yourselfers and more affordable for the average homeowner. Also, sprinkler heads have become increasingly more efficient and water-conserving.

In cold-winter climates, it's important to incorporate a drain-down valve at the lowest point in the system. The pipes must be drained each autumn before the weather turns frigid, because if water freezes inside, the pipes can burst.

You may wish to take a scale drawing of the area you want to water to an irrigation supplier, if you're lucky enough to have one nearby. Suppliers who deal with homeown-

ers are usually happy to compile a parts list, draw up a sprinkler layout, and walk their customers through the installation.

Whether you plan the system yourself or rely on a supplier, you must know your water supply's flow rate—the number of gallons per minute (gpm) flowing through your pipes. The easiest method is to time the number of seconds it takes a fully opened faucet to fill a gallon container, then divide that number into 60. If the container fills in 6 seconds, then your flow rate is 10 gpm.

Sprinkler heads come in fixed-height (risers) and pop-up models. The nozzle type determines how the water is distributed: A fan-spray or mister disperses water in an unchanging pattern; a single stream rotor in multiple, stream-like spurts in a moving pattern; an impact rotary in multiple, far-reaching, moving streams; and a bubbler in a heavy flow. The type of head needed varies for each garden situation. Lawns are usually best watered with pop-up fans.

Irrigation catalogs list specifications for sprinkler heads, including gallonage, spray pattern, and radius of coverage. Most can be adjusted to cover a complete circle or part of a circle. On your scale drawing, arrange the heads so that water from each just touches the adjacent heads. When an exact fit isn't possible, it's better to have heads too close than too far apart. Add the total gallonage of the sprinklers and divide the system into sections, so that no single section exceeds 75 percent of your flow rate.

Once you've planned the sprinkler system and obtained all the parts, you're ready for installation. Here's how to install a lawn sprinkler system:

*Step 1:* Plumb a tee into the main water supply. Install a shut-off valve for the system after the tee so that closing down the system for repairs won't cut off water to the house.

*Step 2:* Install a valve manifold (one valve for each section). For an automated system, use remote-control instead of manual valves, and connect them by direct-burial electrical wire to the controller.

*Step 3:* Dig trenches for the pipe. In an existing lawn, cut the sod and lay it aside before trenching, then replace it when you finish installing the system.

*Step 4:* Install PVC pipe. (Lay it below the frost line in cold-winter climates so it won't heave out of the ground.) Use PVC cement to join pipe and fittings; let the connections harden for 24 hours. Cap off all openings, then test for leaks.

*Step 5:* Install risers (swing joints are stronger than stationary risers) and pop-up sprinkler heads. Check spray patterns before filling in the trenches.

## How Much to Water

You can't just water once and forget it, because moisture evaporates from the soil and is also used by the plants. Every time you irrigate, you're replacing this lost moisture. The amount of water that must be replaced depends on the weather, light conditions, soil type, and plants. Hot, dry, windy, and sunny locations dry out faster than cool, humid, calm, and shady ones, and sandy soils lose water faster than clayey soils. Large plants with extensive root systems use more water than small ones with limited roots, although the latter must be irrigated more often to prevent them from drying out.

The chart on page 35 lists the water needs (combined rainfall and irrigation) of lawns in various climates. Adjust the figures for other plant-ings. Generally, established trees and shrubs need less water than lawns, and established drought-tolerant plantings need supplemental watering only during prolonged dry spells.

Using the gallon figures is easy if you have a drip or permanent in-ground sprinkler system, since gallonage is clearly marked on emitters and sprinkler heads. To figure out inches with above-ground sprinklers, scatter flat-bottomed containers around the planting and see how long the water must run for an inch to collect in each container. (This is also a good way to determine if your sprinklers are putting out an even amount of water.)

Determine how many gallons your garden hose delivers by connecting the nozzle you intend to

<hr>

## Timers and Controllers

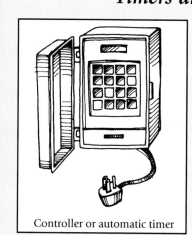

Controller or automatic timer

Whether you choose a drip system or a traditional in-ground system, you'll need one of these devices to automate the watering. The simplest device is a timer that requires you to turn on the water and then shuts it off after a preset length of time. The next step up is a battery-operated device that turns the water on and off at programmed times. You can attach either of these to a faucet to control a portable sprinkler, porous hose, or drip system. Here's where a Y-connector comes in handy: Keep the timer attached to one leg of the Y, and use the other leg as needed for hand-watering.

The most sophisticated controller is one attached by underground low-voltage wire to a multiple-section drip or lawn sprinkler system. Once programmed, the controller turns each valve on, runs it for a preset length of time, then turns it off. It can be connected to a rain sensor, which overrides the system when water isn't needed.

The best timers and controllers allow you to water individual zones for different lengths of time and on different schedules, so that you can deliver the right amount of water to each type of planting. Such a timer is essential if you're automatically watering shrub borders and lawn, since their water needs are vastly different. For a drip system, you'll need a timer that allows you to deliver water to each zone for as long as 6 hours per zone.

Do not preset the timer and ignore it for months on end, unless it has a rain sensor. Instead, you should decide, based on weather conditions, when water is needed and turn the system on only when necessary. That way, you avoid watering during a rainfall or cool, cloudy weather.

*Drip irrigation is the easiest and best way to water beds and borders. The latest clog-free emitters and flexible tubing make a drip-irrigation system easy to install and use. Once the tubing is laid down, it should be camouflaged with a layer of mulch.*

use, turning the faucet to the desired flow, and filling a gallon bucket. If it takes 30 seconds to fill, then you know that to apply 15 gallons would take 7½ minutes (450 seconds): 15 gallons x 30 seconds per gallon = 450 seconds; 450 seconds ÷ 60 seconds per minute = 7½ minutes.

To calculate inches of water from your hose, remember that it takes roughly 62 gallons to apply a 1-inch depth of water over 100 square feet. If you adjust the flow to fill a gallon bucket in 30 seconds (2 gallons a minute), then applying 62 gallons takes 31 minutes.

## Drip Irrigation Systems

Technically, drip irrigation refers to a system that releases water in *drips*, but the term has grown to include any low-pressure system that applies water slowly in gallons per hour (gph) rather than gallons per minute (gpm) as automated lawn sprinklers do. Drip has many benefits: The slow, steady application of water promotes healthy plant growth; drip is water-conserving; and do-it-yourselfers can easily set up and add onto or reroute systems.

Recent improvements in drip technology have eliminated many of the negatives once associated with

the systems, such as the tendency of components to pull apart or emitters to clog. You can count on modern brand-name drip systems to function well and remain clog free. The only major problem might be animals gnawing through the tubing in search of water during dry spells. You might be able to avoid this by providing a small wildlife pool or birdbath in your landscape.

A drip system can include misters, mini-sprayers, and mini-sprinklers, in addition to drip emitters. Since a drip system dispenses water slowly in a small area, it is suitable for all plantings except a lawn—although in the future, new developments in in-line emitter tubing may work for newly planted lawns.

### Drip Components

A drip system begins at the main assembly, which normally includes a valve, backflow preventer, optional fertilizer injector, filter, and pressure regulator. The main line leading from this assembly usually branches into lateral lines leading to different plantings.

Older-model drip systems dispensed water through holes punched in a solid drip hose or through smaller spaghetti tubing capped by emitters. A newer and better type of drip hose with preinstalled in-line emitters represents the biggest advance in drip irrigation in recent years. This is the easiest kind of drip system to install and maintain, and the most problem free.

To keep a drip system in good working order, flush the lines at the beginning of each growing season and at least once during the season. Clean the filter on the same schedule. To safeguard the system in a cold-winter climate, bring the main assembly and battery-controlled

timer indoors. You can leave the drip hose in place, as long as you protect it with a thick layer of mulch.

**Do-It-Yourself Drip Irrigation**

A drip system with in-line emitters is the simplest type to set up and maintain. The drip hose already contains clog-proof emitters embedded inside, so you don't have to punch holes for emitters, mess with spaghetti tubing, or worry about parts snapping off.

The drip hose is available with ½- or 1-gph emitters spaced every 12, 18, 24, or 36 inches apart. For most home landscapes, experts recommend that emitters be spaced 12 inches apart in sandy soil and up to 24 inches apart in clayey soil.

Here are directions for installing a simple drip system in a mixed border. It doesn't matter whether the border is already planted or whether you plant (carefully!) after laying the drip lines:

*Step 1:* Put together the main assembly—valve, backflow preventer, optional fertilizer injector, filter, and pressure regulator—or start with a preassembled unit from a kit. (Proper installation of an injector is vital to protect the drinking water; consult your local building department.) Put a battery-operated timer at the top to automate the system. Attach the assembly to a faucet, which can serve as your valve, or plumb it into your water supply line.

*Step 2:* Run a solid drip hose from the main assembly to the planting area.

*Step 3:* Lay out a drip hose containing in-line emitters in roughly parallel lines on top of the soil. Keep emitters 6 to 12 inches away from plant stems to prevent rotting.

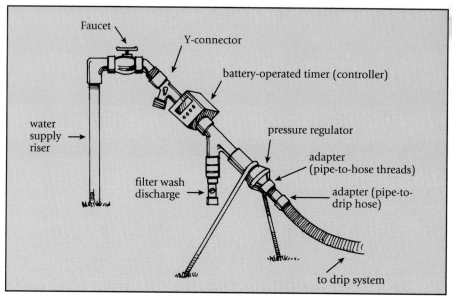

*A drip irrigation system can be hooked directly to an outside faucet. Use a Y-connector so you can also attach a hose or fill a watering can from the faucet.*

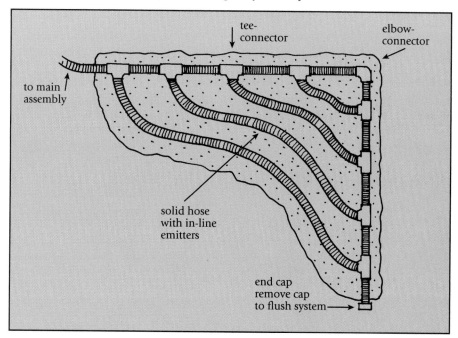

*Do-it-yourselfers can install a drip irrigation system in a landscape. It's easy to lay out hoses, even in irregularly shaped beds, by using either tee- or elbow-connectors.*

*Step 4:* Use elbows and tees to join the lines. Secure the hose to the ground with U-shaped landscape stakes.

*Step 5:* Before attaching end closures, flush the lines by running water through them for at least 5 minutes.

*Step 6:* Mulch around the plants and over the drip hose.

**Less Work Weeding**

Weeding can be one of the most relentless, time-consuming tasks in landscape maintenance, but it does not have to be. You can effectively and easily prevent weeds from estab-

lishing themselves in your yard by depriving them of a place to grow. And if you act quickly to eradicate any weeds that do sneak in, you'll prevent them from reproducing and becoming an even bigger problem.

**Weed Prevention**

Weed seeds that are already present in soil germinate readily when they're near the soil surface and warmed by the sun. It's easy to prevent those lurking weed seeds from sprouting into a problem by shading and cooling the soil with a thick blanket of ground-covering plants

or mulch, or with paving. Low-growing groundcover plants are especially useful as underplantings in flower and shrub borders, where they discourage weeds from sprouting and give the planting an elegant appearance. Never leave the soil bare—cover it with either dense-growing plants or a blanket of weed-deterring mulch. (See page 32 for more information about mulching.)

Avoid using sheets of black plastic or weed barrier cloth or landscape fabric—the kind that allows water and air to penetrate to the soil beneath—in flower and shrub borders, even though the cloth is promoted for such use. Roots of trees and shrubs adhere to the cloth and are damaged when it is removed. (Black plastic sheets are impermeable to water and can cook plant roots.) Also, wood chips or other organic mulch must be layered on top of the cloth or plastic mulch or the UV rays in sunlight will cause them to deteriorate. This defeats the purpose of the weed cloth, since a thick layer of mulch is enough to deter weeds on its own. And if you don't replace the organic mulch as it decomposes on top of the barrier, weeds may germinate there and adhere to the fabric, which will rip when you tug on the weeds.

Weed cloth works well, however, in seasonal plantings such as vegetable gardens, and makes a lot of sense as a barrier beneath gravel or stone paths, patios, and driveways. A layer of weed barrier cloth between the stones and the soil prevents the stones from working their way into the soil and "disappearing." It also stops weeds from germinating, saving you and your knuckles from the task of pulling weeds lodged in the gravel.

You can take other measures to keep weeds out of brick or flagstone patios and walkways. Either mortar the joints, or plant them with small-scale groundcovers or "paving plants" that tolerate some foot traffic. Favorite paving plants include fragrant herbs such as thyme, chamomile, and pinks.

## Eradicating Weeds

Inevitably, some weeds will sprout in your garden regardless of your efforts to keep them out. It's vital to

get rid of them while they're young, before they gain a firm foothold. Not all weeds can be killed the same way, so it's good to know what kind you're dealing with. By learning to recognize weeds, you'll also avoid plucking out seedlings of desirable plants by mistake. Ask your local nursery or agricultural extension office for help in identifying weeds.

Weeds are classified like any other plants. There are herbaceous annual, biennial, and perennial weeds, as well as woody ones. Annual and biennial weeds are easily killed by hoeing, but lopping off the top of a perennial weed does little good, since the plant resprouts from its roots. Some of the most persistent perennial weeds spread by underground stems.

You can eradicate weeds manually or with herbicides (weed killers). Whichever method you choose, do it before the weed spreads out of control or makes seeds. Most weeds produce thousands of seeds, which may germinate right away or remain dormant until the soil is disturbed.

You can get rid of weed seeds manually before planting a bed or border. Till and water the soil to encourage the seeds to sprout, then about two weeks after the initial tilling, when weeds blanket the soil, slice them off at ground level with a hoe or with another shallow tilling. However, it's easier to plant immediately after tilling and then apply a thick weed-deterring layer of mulch on the bare soil before the weeds appear. Mulch applied after weeds germinate may not control them.

When pulling weeds by hand, be sure to do so when the soil is moist—they'll come out more easily than in dry soil.

## Weed Killers

Weed killers (herbicides) offer an efficient way to eradicate weeds in any area, large or small. There are various types of weed killers for different situations, so choosing an appropriate product is important. Keep in mind that herbicides do not know the difference between a weed and a desirable garden plant, so use them very carefully. Never use herbicides frivolously—reserve their use for when you really need

them. And be sure to take appropriate precautions to prevent getting the herbicide on your skin or breathing it.

*Contact herbicides* affect the part of the plant they touch, while *systemic herbicides* are taken up by plant roots and distributed throughout the plant. Systemics are useful in killing weeds that spread rampantly by underground roots or stems. Some weed killers are *selective*, killing only certain types of plants, while *nonselective* types kill indiscriminately. For example, a broad-leaf herbicide can be used in a lawn, because it kills only broadleaf weed plants, such as dandelions, without harming narrow-leaf lawn grasses. Glyphosate, one of the herbicides most commonly used by home gardeners, is a systemic herbicide that affects any plant you spray it on. It does not travel in the soil and quickly breaks down, so is relatively safe to use.

Most weed killers are *post-emergent*—you apply them on growing weeds. Some are *pre-emergent*—you apply them before planting, to kill weed seeds as they germinate. Pre-emergent herbicides are useful in preventing weeds in newly tilled and planted landscapes and for controlling crabgrass in lawns—but timing is crucial in their effectiveness. Follow label directions exactly to avoid harming valued plants.

## Weeding Tools

Various tools are available to help you control weeds manually and with herbicides. Here is an overview of the most helpful implements:

*Hoes and Cultivators* The common garden hoe has a square blade, which is used to slice off weeds at the soil. Cultivators usually have

SHEARING

hedge shears

new growth only near stem tips

*Pruning evergreen shrubs with hedge shears results in flat-sided, formal-looking plants. Shearing stimulates rapid growth only near the cut ends of the stems, while the shrubs' centers are usually devoid of leaves. The rapid growth means you must shear repeatedly every year to keep the plants looking neat.*

THINNING

hand-held clippers

new growth from along length of stem

*Thinning an evergreen shrub with one-handed clippers, by removing lengths of stems from where they branch in the shrub's interior, controls size without stimulating excessive growth. The resulting growth is natural-looking and dense, with leaves deep in the shrub's center. Thinned shrubs grow slowly and need pruning only once every year or two.*

prongs or tines to snag weeds and pull them loose. These long-handled tools are useful for killing newly sprouted weeds in areas of bare soil, such as vegetable gardens, but not in beds blanketed with mulch or groundcovers. Use caution when hoeing around a shrub or tree, because you can easily damage their roots.

*Hand Weeders* These include various implements for uprooting weeds and are essential when dealing with perennial weeds that grow back from any bit of root left in the soil. Among the most useful of these tools is the asparagus knife, also known as a dandelion weeder. Stick the long metal probe with its forked end into the ground under the roots and pry the weed loose.

*Tank Sprayers* A tank sprayer is the safest way to apply liquid herbicide over a large area. (It is much safer than a hose-end sprayer, which shoots weed killer in a wide arc.) A tank sprayer used for applying weed killers shouldn't be used for other purposes, since the chemical residue can contaminate other materials. Mark it clearly with the words "Herbicides Only." Spray only on calm days when the temperature is below 85°F, to prevent herbicide drift.

To operate this type of compression sprayer, put weed killer in the tank, dilute with water as directed, pump the piston to get air into the tank, and then squeeze the trigger on the wand to dispense the herbicide through the nozzle. A plastic unit is much lighter than a metal one, and it won't corrode. Tank sprayers for home gardens usually come in capacities of 1 to 3 gallons. Get one that won't be too heavy for you to carry around when it's full,

and make sure the nozzle can be adjusted from a stream to a fine mist.

*Spreaders* The same spreader used for fertilizing a lawn can be used to apply granular weed killers. Since the herbicide is dry, you don't have to worry about contamination, as you do with a tank sprayer or hose-end sprayer. (See page 34 for information about the various types of spreaders.)

## Less Work Pruning

You can drastically reduce pruning chores by following two simple steps: First, choose plants suited to

the space you have allotted them. That way, you won't waste time cutting back plants that get tangled together, spread over walkways, and obscure windows. Second, let the plants grow naturally. That means allowing a plant to assume its natural shape rather than imposing a shape on it by your pruning method. Shearing shrubs into flat-sided hedges or into cones, squares, and other geometric shapes actually creates more work, because it encourages faster growth. These formal shapes need constant maintenance, since any little bit of wayward growth ruins their appearance.

<table>
<tr><td>

**RIGHT**

before pruning    after thinning

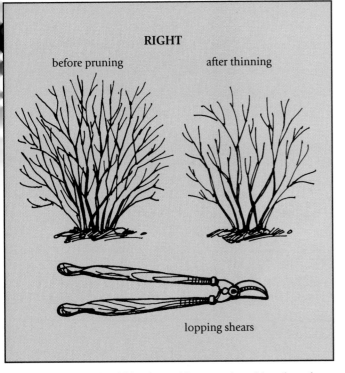

lopping shears

</td><td>

**WRONG**

before pruning    after shearing

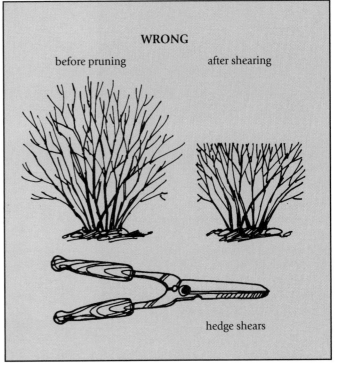

hedge shears

</td></tr>
</table>

*Deciduous shrubs should be thinned by removing old and weak branches from near ground level with loppers or a pruning saw. Ends of branches may also be cut back to branch crotches with hand-held clippers. This pruning method retains the shrub's natural, graceful shape while controlling growth. Thinned shrubs need pruning only every few years.*

*Do not prune deciduous shrubs into geometrical shapes with hedge shears, unless you intend to create a formal hedge. This type of pruning causes excessive growth that necessitates repeat pruning and destroys a shrub's natural form.*

Many fine plants need some pruning, so don't expect to avoid the task altogether. But remember, how you trim the plant makes all the difference in the way it grows and how much pruning it will need in the future. The most important technique in maintaining shrubs in a low-maintenance landscape is to *thin rather than shear.* Heeding that advice will save you a lot of work in the long run.

### Thinning Versus Shearing

*Thinning* (done with the kind of clippers you hold in one hand) allows a plant to grow naturally at its own pace, making less work for you. *Shearing* (usually done with two-handled hedge clippers) clips a plant into an unnatural shape, resulting in rapid growth and the need for more frequent pruning. Sheared plants usually have thin shells of exterior foliage and leafless interiors. Thinned shrubs are dense, with more interior leaves and a fluffier appearance.

Thinning is the pruning method recommended for shrubs and trees in low-maintenance landscapes. It reduces the plant's size and directs branches where you want them to go without stimulating a lot of new growth. While the actual thinning process may take longer than shearing, it needs to be repeated less often—saving you time in the long run. And thinned shrubs have a longer landscape life than sheared ones.

To thin evergreen or deciduous shrubs, cut the branches back to their points of origin on the main trunk or to where they form a Y with another branch. With most deciduous shrubs, you should also saw off old and weak stems at ground level to encourage new growth from the base of the plant. You can keep a shrub at a desirable size simply by thinning it every year or two—usually in the spring immediately after blooming, to direct the season's growth.

Shearing indiscriminately removes short lengths of top growth, often leaving stubs. Since this type of pruning removes all the buds on the stem tips, it encourages a profusion of new growth behind the cuts from buds farther down the stems. Soon you have to shear again to contain that growth, which in turn stimulates a new flush of growth. You must keep shearing several times a year to maintain the neat appearance of the shrub or hedge. (Thinning removes fewer buds and thus doesn't stimulate as much new growth.) Shearing is suitable only for formal, flat-sided hedges, not for shrubs in low-maintenance landscapes.

### The Time to Prune

The time of year you prune flowering shrubs makes a difference, since you want to encourage blossoms, not cut them off. If you're pruning a spring-blooming shrub, hold off until immediately after flowering. Prune by midsummer and avoid pruning in fall, since buds for spring blossoms are formed in mid- to late summer. Summer-flowering shrubs usually bloom on new growth formed that same year, so they can be pruned in late winter or early spring (or immediately after blooming) without sacrificing flowers.

## Pruning Tools

Making sharp, clean cuts is important when you're pruning, so you're wise to invest in a few good tools. (Never force a pruning tool to cut a larger-diameter branch than it's designed to handle—you risk ruining the cutting edge and forcing the blades out of alignment, while butchering the plant in the process.) Here's an overview of the various pruning tools available:

*Handheld Pruners* These pruners are intended to cut stems up to ½ inch in diameter. There are two basic designs: *scissor pruners*, which have two sharpened, overlapping blades; and *anvil pruners*, which have a sharpened blade that crushes the stem against a metal anvil. Scissor pruners make cleaner, closer cuts than anvil models. Since handheld pruners get frequent use, it pays to buy good-quality ones with steel blades, since they stay sharp longer. Choose pruners that feel comfortable in your hand when you operate them. Beware of any that open very wide, since these can tire your hand.

*Loppers* These long-handled pruners provide extra leverage for cutting branches up to 1½ inches in diameter. They're especially handy for removing branches at the base of deciduous shrubs. Like handheld pruners, loppers are available in scissor and anvil models. Again, scissor types are recommended for neater cuts.

*Pruning Saws* A saw is recommended for branches with larger diameters than handheld pruners or loppers can handle. A small curved saw is adequate for most tasks, and it's useful for getting into tight spots. A folding model is a good choice—when the saw is closed, you can

*Using a mulching mower greatly reduces the time spent on lawn care, and it's good for the lawn, too! Grass clippings are cut up so small, they settle between the grass blades—not on the lawn surface—where they quickly decay and nourish the lawn. And you don't have to empty a grass catcher and find a way to dispose of all the clippings.*

carry it around safely, and the blade is protected. Unless you plan to get into tree pruning, you won't need the bigger models or those mounted on poles.

*Hedge Shears* These two-handled, scissor-bladed tools are designed for cutting shrubs into flat walls or formal shapes—something to avoid doing in an easy-care landscape. However, you'll find hedge shears handy for cutting back dead tops of perennials and ornamental grasses in late winter. You can remove more of their dead stems in a single snip with the shears than you can with small handheld pruners.

## Less Work Mowing the Lawn

Mowing is the single most time-consuming and repetitive maintenance task, even if you design your lawn to make the job easier. (See page 21.) Beyond planning sensibly, here are some things you can do to lessen the work:

- Avoid giving the lawn too much water or fertilizer. Why make it grow faster if you

*For the best lawn health, be sure to change the blade height on your mower as lawn conditions warrant. It's best to avoid cutting off more than one-third of the length of the grass blades with each mowing, or you could damage the lawn's vigor. Leave grass in a shady yard longer than in a sunny spot.*

really want to mow less often? Overly lush growth can also make the lawn more prone to pests and diseases.

- Don't waste time mowing grass that grows poorly—get rid of it. For example, if you have to keep reseeding a shady corner, replace the grass in that spot with a shade-tolerant planting that you don't have to pamper.

- Some mowing patterns are more efficient than others. You can save time and energy by mowing in a continuous circular pattern. That way, you won't have to turn the mower 180 degrees time and time again, as you do when mowing in parallel paths. First, mow the perimeter of the lawn, rounding off any square corners. Then cut the remainder of the lawn in a spiral until you end up in the middle.

- You can also trim mowing time by using a mower with the widest cutting width

## Seasonal Mowing Tips for Easy Lawn Care

Grass grows at different rates during the year, depending on the temperature and the amount of moisture and fertilizer it gets. For best lawn health, mow Northern grasses shorter when they're actively growing, and leave them longer when they're growing slowly. Southern grasses need to be left longer during summer to protect them from the heat. The table below provides some guidance on where to set your mower's cutting height.

### RECOMMENDED BLADE SETTINGS

|  | Spring & Fall | Summer* |
|---|---|---|
| **Northern Grasses** | | |
| Buffalograss | 1½ in. | 2½ in. |
| Fine fescue | 1½ in. | 2 in. |
| Kentucky bluegrass | 2½ in. | 3 in. |
| Perennial ryegrass | 1½ in. | 2½ in. |
| Tall fescue | 2⅕ in. | 4 in. |
| **Southern Grasses** | | |
| Bahiagrass | 2 in. | 3 in. |
| Bermudagrass | ½ in. | 1 in. |
| Centipede grass | 1 in. | 2 in. |
| St. Augustine grass | 2 in. | 3 in. |

*Summer refers to the period of time when temperatures remain consistently above 80°F or when rainfall drops off dramatically.*

possible. Choose a width that suits your budget, strength, and lawn size and shape. Mowing ¼ acre of lawn with an 18-inch-wide blade requires about 2 miles of walking. Using a 21-inch-wide blade reduces the number of laps, saving you about ½ mile. A mowing strip around the perimeter of the lawn can also save you time, since it eliminates the need to trim the edge separately.

■ Leaving grass clippings on the lawn is not only a time saver, but also good for the lawn—as long as the clippings are short. In fact, environmentalists have coined a name for the practice: grass-cycling. The clippings eventually decompose, thus improving the soil and reducing the need to fertilize. You can expect clippings to break down within a week to 10 days when they're cut with a mulching mower.

■ Grasses predominant in the North grow rapidly during cool weather in spring and fall, while Southern types are more active in summer. Set the height of your mower blades to reflect these seasonal growth patterns. Regardless of the season, however, whenever you mow, avoid stressing the lawn by removing more than one-third of the grass's length each time you mow. (See the chart above for proper mowing height). If you ordinarily mow your lawn shorter than the recommended heights, keep in mind that a high-mown lawn is healthier and more weed resistant than a closely clipped one. If a lawn is mowed too short during hot weather, the roots suffer and weeds quickly invade—causing more work for you!

### Mower Choices

No matter how much you streamline mowing, you'll still have to push around a lawn mower more than you probably want to. At the very least, get a mower that makes the job more tolerable. Whichever type you choose, be sure you can easily adjust the cutting height.

*Reel Mowers* These old-fashioned people-powered mowers have matured into modern types made from lightweight materials, so they're easier to push than they used to be. They're also blissfully quiet compared to power mowers. Reel mowers have narrower blades than most power mowers, so it takes more passes to cover the same territory. Still, a reel mower is a nice choice for a small lawn, as long as the lawn doesn't collect a lot of twigs or leaves—the mower can't handle these, nor can it handle tall grass.

If you like the human-powered approach and have only occasional litter, you may want to use a reel mower and rake if needed before mowing. Also, consider a reel mower if you want your kids to mow the lawn—there's less chance of accidents than with power mowers.

*Conventional Power Mowers* These are called conventional to distinguish them from mulching mowers. (See page 46.) They blow the cut grass out a discharge chute at the side or rear, while a mulching mower chops the grass and distributes it evenly over the lawn. Rear baggers are better balanced than side baggers, and allow close cutting on both sides of the mower. For versatility, the mower should have a convertible side chute discharge to use when you're not bagging.

With a conventional model, you'll have to haul and empty the bag of clippings, and you'll need a convenient way to dispose of them. Or, you could leave the clippings on the lawn, where they break down and return nutrients to the soil. However, clippings left behind by conventional mowers can cause many problems. For example, clippings

*A leaf blower won't replace a rake for removing leaves from a lawn, but it's handy for blowing them off of hard surfaces such as decks, patios, and driveways.*

can spray all over walks and flower borders if you fail to aim the chute toward the center of the lawn. You may also leave unsightly and unhealthy clumps of clippings on the lawn if the grass is on the long side when you cut it. Long clippings are easily tracked into the house, adding further to clean-up chores. To avoid these problems, use a mulching mower. (See below.)

You can choose from gasoline-powered, electric, and battery-charged types. Gasoline models are designed for the heaviest duty, while electric and battery types are adequate for small lawns. Test the engine to be sure it starts up easily. Variable speeds are desirable for controlling your pace. A blade-brake-clutch will stop the blade without killing the engine. Make sure the handle feels comfortable and that the mower is easy to push. If pushing requires too much muscle, get a self-propelled model that needs only to be steered.

As far as safety is concerned, all recent models must meet government standards. That standard says that the mower's spinning blade must stop spinning within three seconds of releasing the mower's handle. Mowers with a blade-brake-clutch cost more but are easier to use because the engine doesn't stop when you stop the blade. Other mowers have an "engine-kill control," which stops both the engine and the blade. This is inconvenient, since you must restart the engine each time you want to stop the mower.

*Mulching Mowers* Instead of discharging whole clippings through a chute, a mulching power mower chops them up and deposits the pieces evenly over the lawn. This process not only saves you time, it also improves lawn health by returning nitrogen to the soil. Mulching mowers also chop up fallen leaves into such fine pieces that they can be spewed back on the lawn as an organic soil amendment.

These mowers have been around since the 1970s, but new models have been designed for better performance and efficiency. All major mower companies now offer mulching models. (Converter kits, which supposedly turn conventional mowers into mulching mowers, usually give disappointing results.)

Look for a mulching mower with at least a 4½- to 5-horsepower motor, since the blade must operate at high speed to mulch efficiently. If you want a dedicated mulching mower, look for one with a doughnut-shaped housing—that's a good sign that you'll get a good mulching cut. But if you plan to bag grass clippings or fallen leaves for your compost pile, consider a model that converts from mulching to conventional mowing with a bagging attachment. Make sure that the process for changing from one type of mowing to another is simple and convenient.

*Riding Mowers* You need at least a half-acre of lawn to justify buying one of these expensive machines. They offer many options, which push up the base price considerably. Although riding mowers are a quick, comfortable way to mow huge lawns, the wide turning radius on most models makes them inefficient in curves and other tight spots— you may also need a regular power mower to handle those areas.

## Less Work Cleaning Up

Even in an easy-care landscape, you'll need to perform some regular cleanup chores. Here are some tried-and-true methods and tools to make the job easier:

### Dispatching Fallen Leaves

Dealing with fallen leaves is by far the biggest cleanup chore facing home gardeners in areas where deciduous trees and shrubs abound. Lawns need to be raked clean of fallen leaves, but leaves need not always be removed from beds and borders unless they are unsightly. For example, leaves that fall into groundcovers such as pachysandra often shift to the ground beneath the evergreen covering during winter and decay there, enriching the soil. So you need not be scrupulous about removing leaf litter from groundcovers unless it makes a smothering blanket. Also, it's not necessary— or desirable—to sweep up litter in a naturalistic landscape.

The easiest way to deal with leaves on the lawn is to mow them along with the grass during most of the growing season, especially if you have a mulching or bagging mower. In fall, when leaves blanket the lawn, you can simplify cleanup by mowing the leaves and bagging them along with grass clippings if you have a conventional mower. A mulching mower crumbles dry leaves into fine pieces that fall down between the grass blades. Rake leaves from flower beds and shrub borders and "mow" them up, or collect them on a garden tarp or in a garden tote bag, and take them to a central pile for bagging or shredding.

*Leaf Rakes* These lightweight rakes have plastic, metal, or bamboo tines that fan out from a long wooden handle. Use them for pulling leaves and other debris off the lawn and out of garden beds. Although bamboo tines aren't as durable as plastic or metal ones, they're gentler on plants. Rake heads come in various sizes—a wide head is ideal for

*Using a mulching mower on a leaf-strewn lawn saves time in more ways than one. For instance, you can cut the grass and "rake" leaves at the same time. The mower chops leaves so finely that they settle to the ground and decay into lawn-nourishing mulch. And you don't have to empty the leaf catcher as you would with a traditional mower, or bag leaves, as you would if you raked the lawn.*

raking a large quantity of leaves into piles, and a narrow one for getting into tight spaces.

*Leaf Blowers* Instead of wielding a broom or leaf rake, you can use one of these machines to clear patios, driveways, walkways, and other areas of leaves and dirt. (They aren't meant for use on lawns—a conventional rake does the job much faster.) Handheld models are popular among homeowners, while backpack models are commonly used by professional maintenance crews. Aim the blower at debris and gather it into piles for bagging. Some types vacuum up leaves and shred them, but you'll probably lack the time and patience to use this machine for anything but small shredding jobs. For big jobs, use a leaf shredder. (See below.)

Using a leaf blower isn't always a pleasant experience—the machines can be extremely noisy, and the vibration makes them tiring to hold onto. Unless the machine is well balanced, it may tire your hand and back. Try out any models you're considering and test for weight, balance, and noise level, if possible. Electric types are quieter than gas models, but if you have obstacles in

your way, the cord may get tangled and become annoying. Neither gas nor electric models handle wet leaves very well.

*Leaf Shredders and Power Mowers* There are several types of gas-powered or electric machines designed to shred leaves: the leaf blowers mentioned above (they have a vacuum that sucks up leaves and a blade inside that shreds them); dedicated models that do nothing but shred; and chipper/shredders that chop leaves in one part of the machine and chip wood in another part.

The dedicated shredder is more efficient than combination machines, which shred extremely slowly. It has a wide-mouthed hopper for accepting lots of leaves, and it chews them as fast as you can load them in. The hopper can sit on its own base, or atop a garbage can. Be sure to wear eye protection when using any of these machines, and follow the manufacturer's directions carefully.

You might not want to invest in a fancy leaf shredder to chop up leaves if you have a power lawn mower with good suction and lots of horsepower. (A mulching mower should be convertible so that you can switch to conventional mow-

ing using a bagger; see page 46.) Just mow the leaf-strewn lawn and gather the clippings and chewed up leaves in the grass catcher. You can chop the leaves even finer by emptying the bag on the driveway and mowing and bagging the pile again. The shredded leaves make excellent mulch or can be composted.

*Chipper/Shredders* These machines are supposed to reduce all sorts of debris—leaves, brush, and clippings—into small pieces. The branches go into a side chute for chipping, and the leaves and garden waste go into a large upright hopper for shredding. In fact, they shred very slowly, since the hopper is much smaller than on a dedicated leaf shredder. You can get a type with a large leaf-holding attachment, but the leaves tend to clog as they go through the narrow opening into the machine.

These machines do a better job of chipping branches. The best electric models chip branches up to 1½ inches in diameter, while top-quality, gasoline-powered types handle diameters up to 3 inches. The bigger the branch capacity, the more expensive the machine. But most machines handle only straight branches—crooked or knobby branches pose problems. These machines can be very dangerous and should be used with extreme caution and according to manufacturer's directions.

Ask yourself whether you really need such large, costly equipment. If your municipality collects brush and chips it for you, even if only once or twice a year, why not let them do the job? If you hire a professional tree service to prune your trees, they will chip the prunings and leave them for you.

*Turning yard waste into useful compost can be a rewarding part of gardening. It doesn't require a lot of labor if you use the cold composting method and allow the materials to decay on their own without turning them.*

## Ecological Composting

A ready supply of homemade compost—that rich, dark, earthy substance that remains when organic matter decays—is indispensable for mulching and improving the soil. Making compost is often considered a laborious, time-consuming task, but it doesn't have to be. Properly planned, composting won't overextend even an easy-care gardener. You can easily produce your own compost from garden trimmings, fallen leaves, grass clippings, other yard waste, and kitchen scraps. And since many communities no longer collect yard waste at the curb, it makes environmental sense to recycle it at home.

Compost is simply decayed organic matter. The matter decays when it's consumed by various organisms, ranging from microscopic fungi and bacteria to plainly visible earthworms and sow bugs. The more favorable the conditions, the faster the organisms produce compost. Their activity heats up the pile, further speeding decay. The organisms need plenty of air, enough moisture so the pile is damp throughout, and a mixture of carbon- and nitrogen-rich waste.

Carbonaceous materials are brown or dry, such as fallen leaves and twigs; nitrogenous materials are green or fresh, such as grass clippings and rotten vegetables. Although layering green and dry ingredients is traditional, mixing the pieces is actually more effective. Scientists recommend creating a pile with a high ratio, by weight, of carbon to nitrogen, but no home gardener can be expected to estimate quantities on that basis. Roughly equal volumes of green and brown types of waste should do the job. The smaller the pieces of waste, the faster they'll decay—put them through a shredder if you have one and are anxious for quick compost.

Decomposition occurs on its own, given enough time, but you can speed up the process. When you intervene to provide the organisms with good conditions—usually by regularly turning the pile—then you're "managing" the pile. "Passive" or "cold" composting lets nature take its course. You just pile up waste and let it slowly rot on its own. After a year or two, you can begin to retrieve decomposed material from the bottom of the pile.

There's no need to add any amendments to the pile. Compost activators or inoculants are often recommended, but a few handfuls of garden soil or old compost provide just as many compost-making microbes. If the pile fails to decay, it usually means you must add more

*A no-labor way to aerate a compost pile, and thus speed up decomposition, is to insert PVC pipe with holes drilled into it throughout the compost pile. Shake the pipes every once in a while to let in additional air.*

fresh material or moisture; and an overpowering smell means more dry material and air is needed.

## Easier Composting

Many gardeners mistakenly believe that a compost pile needs regular labor-intensive turning to get it to heat up. Actually, the purpose of turning the pile is to introduce air—one of the key ingredients needed by the organisms for efficient composting. Fortunately, there are less taxing ways to aerate a compost pile than turning it by hand.

One of the easiest methods is to construct the pile on a wooden pallet or a plastic aeration mat sold by some composting equipment suppliers. Or you can drill holes in a 1-inch-diameter PVC pipe and set it upright in the middle of the pile to let in air. Another labor-saving method is to place lengths of drilled PVC pipe horizontally throughout the pile and shake the ends periodically to let in air. (See illustration on page 48.)

A manufactured compost tumbler is another way, though an expensive one, to let in air and save labor. All you do is turn the crank to rotate the pile. The more often you turn the tumbler, the faster you'll get finished compost.

A compost pile can be freestanding—there's no real need for a bin, except to keep the stack of material neat. If you opt for a bin, you can construct your own. It doesn't have to be fancy—a simple hoop made from chicken wire does the trick. Or you can buy one of the many types of plastic, wood, and metal bins available nowadays.

Whatever method you choose, keep in mind that for efficient composting, the pile should be neither too large nor too small. A 3-by-3- to 4-by-4-foot pile is the best size. Most bins on the market are smaller than this, so shop wisely.

Many gardeners like to have three bins side by side for ease of use: One holds finished, ready-to-use compost; the other two are for compost in the making. You can fork the decaying matter easily from one bin to the other to speed its decomposition, or make cold compost in each of the three bins in a three-year cycle, since it can take several years

*Container gardens look attractive on a front porch or patio, but need a lot of attention because they quickly dry out. However, when hooked up to a drip irrigation system, a container garden practically takes care of itself.*

for thorough decomposition if you don't turn the pile.

## Less Work Growing in Containers

Container gardening is considered high maintenance, because the flowering plants commonly grown in containers need extra water and fertilizer. A few simple steps will take much of the work out of caring for plants grown in containers.

For example, plants will go longer between waterings when they're in nonporous or large containers. Water won't evaporate through a nonporous material such as glazed pottery, as it does from a porous one such as wood or clay. The larger the container, the more potting soil it can hold and the longer the soil takes to dry out once it is moistened. The soil in a gallon container may dry out in hours, while that in a half wine barrel may go for days between waterings. To conserve moisture even longer, you can add water-absorbing gel to a soil mix or line a clay container with plastic.

To make container gardening truly carefree, automate watering with a

drip irrigation system. The containers should be on a separate valve so that you can water them separately from plantings in the ground. You can use in-line emitters (see page 40) in large planter boxes, but individual drip emitters with spaghetti tubing are more practical for smaller pots.

The reason many container gardeners must fertilize so frequently is that they use water-soluble products, which leach out of the container with every watering. To minimize the task of feeding, apply a slow-release fertilizer that remains in the potting soil and breaks down gradually. This is the easiest way to fertilize containerized plants, whether you water by hand or with a drip system.

Once you start using the various work-saving tools and techniques discussed in this chapter, you'll find that yard maintenance can be a manageable and even enjoyable part of home ownership. Best of all, efficient maintenance gives you plenty of leisure time to enjoy your landscape—from a lounge chair or a hammock!

# CHAPTER 3

# Easy-Care Front Yards

*These Professional Designs Create Year-Round Good Looks and Are a Cinch to Maintain*

An attractive, well-designed front yard shows off your home to advantage and is a source of pride for you, your family, and your neighbors. A lovely streetside landscape lifts your spirits every time you come home and makes a wonderful impression on visitors. In addition, a beautiful front yard increases the value of your property, as anyone who has bought or sold a house knows. You'll be pleased to discover that good-looking landscapes do not necessarily demand a lot of upkeep. If properly designed, a landscape can be both beautiful and easy-care.

The 18 front-yard plans presented here are designed to put an attractive public face on your property without demanding much upkeep in return. The plans are developed for a variety of house styles and property sizes, so you're sure to find something suitable, whether your home is cozy and located on a tiny urban plot, or rambling and on a spacious suburban tract. Even if your lot is unusually narrow or shallow, you'll find a plan to make the best of your situation. Although the plans are designed to minimize maintenance, they don't sacrifice good looks for easy care. As you leaf through the following pages, notice how appealing each design is. In fact, each plan proves that low maintenance doesn't have to mean boring!

The designers take great pains in choosing plants that provide a long season of interest and also stay within their allotted space. They select low-growing and dwarf plants that won't overgrow windows and walkways, and favor trees with small or delicate leaves, which break down quickly and take some of the work out of fall leaf cleanup. In addition, the designers include interplantings and mixed plantings to increase each garden's interest and camouflage plants past their peak.

All of the plans feature small or moderate-sized lawns that won't overburden the easy-care gardener—one lacks a lawn altogether. Some designs show work-saving mowing strips or lawn edgings, while others offer them as an option. If you don't want to mow, you can always substitute a low-growing groundcover for turf to reduce maintenance even more.

Design: Ireland-Gannon Associates

*A traditional landscape design can be easy to care for if the lawn is small
and an easy-to-mow shape. Long-blooming, low-maintenance perennials and
trees with small leaflets further reduce maintenance chores.*

# Narrow-Lot Traditional Home

This design shows how much landscape interest can be packed into a tiny lot with a limited front yard and only a few feet of setback on either side of the house. The yard contains all the key features you'd expect to find on a more expansive property, but it doesn't feel crowded. In fact, the design makes the lot seem larger, while its small scale makes it easy to maintain.

A sense of spaciousness is developed by secluding the passage to the house and revealing it in stages as you walk to the door. The designer takes advantage of the rectangular area formed by the juncture of the garage and house to create a private entryway. A charming wooden arbor bearing a flowering vine invites visitors to approach the gated picket fence enclosing the entrance. Once inside, the visitor is surrounded by greenery. To prevent the various elements from looking disjointed, stonework is used in the walk leading from the drive to the front door and on the house facade to tie the design together.

In keeping with the sparseness of the front and side yards, small-scale shrubs, perennials, and groundcovers are used for the foundation and other plantings. Many of these feature colorful foliage, flowers, and fruit, which stand out beautifully against the patches of green lawn. A trio of narrow flowering trees adds dimension to the small lot without overwhelming it. Mulched rings under the lawn trees facilitate mowing.

## Landscape Plan L280 shown in spring

*Designed by Damon Scott*
Home Plan 3379
*For information about ordering blueprints for this home call 1-800-521-6797.*

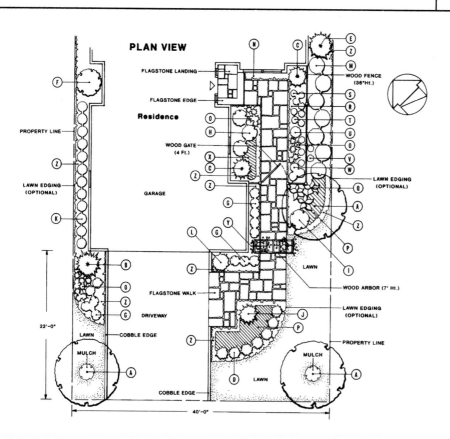

**PLAN VIEW**

FLAGSTONE LANDING

FLAGSTONE EDGE

**Residence**

WOOD GATE
(4 Ft.)

PROPERTY LINE

LAWN EDGING
(OPTIONAL)

GARAGE

FLAGSTONE WALK

DRIVEWAY

LAWN

MULCH

COBBLE EDGE

22'-0"

40'-0"

WOOD FENCE
(36"Ht.)

LAWN EDGING
(OPTIONAL)

WOOD ARBOR (7' Ht.)

LAWN EDGING
(OPTIONAL)

PROPERTY LINE

LAWN

MULCH

LAWN

COBBLE EDGE

## REGIONALIZED PLANT LISTS

Because climate and growing conditions vary greatly throughout North America, it is impossible to list here all the plants for this landscape plan that would do well everywhere on the continent. However, you can order a Blueprint Package with plant lists keyed to this plan and selected by expert horticulturists to thrive in your area.

The six-page Blueprint Package features a large-size version of this Plan View, plus a detailed regional Plant and Materials List. It also includes an illustrated list of hundreds of landscape plants suited to your region, in case you wish to make substitutions, as well as planting instructions and plant adaptation maps to ensure professional results with your new landscape.

See page 157 to order your regionalized Blueprint Package.

*A narrow lot is no excuse for a ho-hum landscape. This design creates a private setting featuring an assortment of easy-care trees, shrubs, perennials, and groundcovers.*

*Brick, flagstone, and a trio of shade trees are used as unifying elements in this easy-care landscape designed for a small lot. The trees balance the size of the house while focusing attention on the main sections of the garden: a curving mixed border, a fence-enclosed terrace, and a narrow grassy strip.*

## REGIONALIZED PLANT LISTS

Because climate and growing conditions vary greatly throughout North America, it is impossible to list here all the plants for this landscape plan that would do well everywhere on the continent. However, you can order a Blueprint Package with plant lists keyed to this plan and selected by expert horticulturists to thrive in your area.

The six-page Blueprint Package features a large-size version of this Plan View, plus a detailed regional Plant and Materials List. It also includes an illustrated list of hundreds of landscape plants suited to your region, in case you wish to make substitutions, as well as planting instructions and plant adaptation maps to ensure professional results with your new landscape.

See page 157 to order your regionalized Blueprint Package.

# Narrow-Lot Contemporary Home

The paving materials and triad of vase-shaped shade trees unify this attractive, easy-care streetside landscape on a fairly tight lot. Brick inlay in the driveway points the way to the walkway that curves around to the porticoed front door at the side of the house. Flagstone on the entrance landing is repeated in the private terrace outside the living room's French doors and in the pavers that lead around the right side of the house to the backyard.

The shade trees form a triangle, each point of which serves a particular design function. The tree to the right of the drive enlivens the narrow strip of lawn and balances the weight of the house. Its underplanting of flowering groundcover and spring bulbs adds color while simplifying mowing. The tree to the far left anchors a curving border containing colorful, small-scale groundcovers, compact shrubs, and easy-care perennials and ornamental grasses. The tree nearest the house screens the small flagstone terrace from public view and furnishes cool shade for anyone seated on the bench.

The landscape includes just enough lawn to offer a soothing, uniform green texture, which provides visual relief from the mixed plantings and contrasts prettily with the brick and flagstone, without demanding a lot of maintenance. The circular sweep of grass flanking the brick walk and mixed border helps break up the generally straight lines of the lawn.

## Landscape Plan L281 shown in summer

*Designed by Maria Morrison*
Home Plan 3485
*For information about ordering blueprints for this home call 1-800-521-6797.*

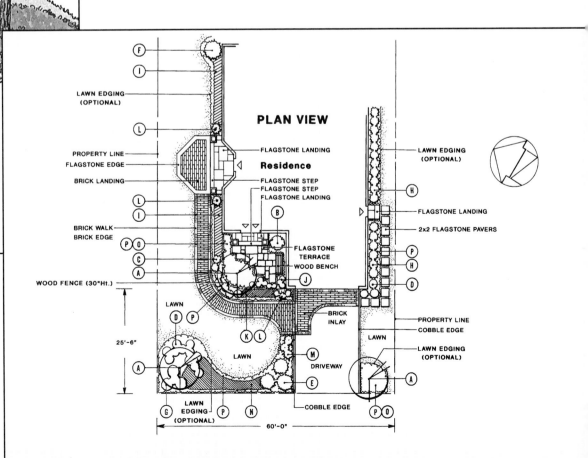

PLAN VIEW

Residence

# Craftsman Home

Although this home sits on a narrow lot with a small front yard and an optional driveway, the designer hasn't skimped on the landscape. The tiny grounds boast a wealth of plants in a striking range of colors, textures, and shapes. The key to successfully landscaping such a small space is to use compact plants that won't outgrow their welcome. Because of the tight quarters, the designer has also chosen to plant a single deciduous tree instead of forming the more traditional triad.

The design has aspects of symmetry and formality—the flagstone walk dividing the yard in half, perennials repeated on either side of the walk, identical pools of lawn, and matching dwarf conifers flanking the porch steps—but the overall effect is informal. Flagstone pavers lead from the walk around the left side of the property only, providing access to cars parked in the driveway. The visual weight of this border balances that of the evergreen tree and cluster of shrubs on the opposite side of the property.

This petite, but lush, landscape requires little effort to maintain, and even the patches of lawn can be cut quickly with a reel mower. However, if you wanted to reduce maintenance even further, you could eliminate the lawn and extend the groundcover. The design may also be adapted to a lot without a driveway or a garage.

## Landscape Plan L282 shown in spring
*Designed by Salvatore A. Masullo*
Home Plan 3316
*For information about ordering blueprints for this home call 1-800-521-6797.*

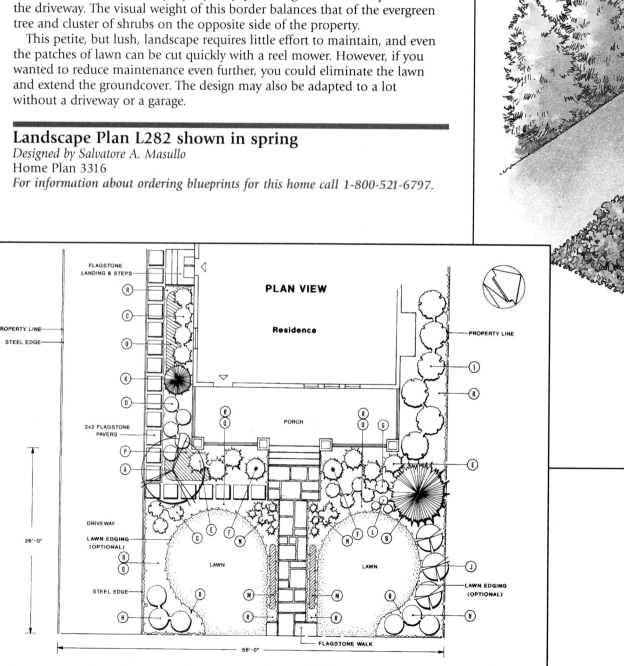

## REGIONALIZED PLANT LISTS

Because climate and growing conditions vary greatly throughout North America, it is impossible to list here all the plants for this landscape plan that would do well everywhere on the continent. However, you can order a Blueprint Package with plant lists keyed to this plan and selected by expert horticulturists to thrive in your area.

The six-page Blueprint Package features a large-size version of this Plan View, plus a detailed regional Plant and Materials List. It also includes an illustrated list of hundreds of landscape plants suited to your region, in case you wish to make substitutions, as well as planting instructions and plant adaptation maps to ensure professional results with your new landscape.

See page 157 to order your regionalized Blueprint Package.

*Eye-catching plantings turn this charming cottage into a special home, yet the yard doesn't demand much upkeep because the plants were chosen for their small size or slow growth.*

# Folk Victorian Home

Graceful, curving foundation plantings really make this landscape! Set against a carpet of green grass, the mixed plantings contain shrubs, perennials, bulbs, and groundcovers chosen for compactness as well as for attractive foliage and flowers. One of a trio of handsome multi-trunked deciduous trees with attractive peeling bark anchors the largest planting. Set near the porch, the tree contributes cool shade during the summer.

The tree to the far left softens the driveway, as do the cobblestones bordering the asphalt. Like the cobbles, the other paving materials—brick and flagstone—are selected for their compatibility with the house style. A brick walk leads to an arching entry landing set at the base of the stairs. The curved landing and planting beds echo the curves in the porch detail and some of the windows. Both the walk and terrace are edged with flagstone, a material repeated in the pavers leading from the opposite side of the driveway to the back of the house.

The third tree in the triangle is planted at the front of the lawn, where its picturesque bark can be admired close up by passersby. At the same time that the tree attracts attention, it also provides some screening and privacy. It is set in a ring of mulch for easy mowing.

## Landscape Plan L283 shown in summer
*Designed by Damon Scott*
Home Plan 2974
*For information about ordering blueprints for this home call 1-800-521-6797.*

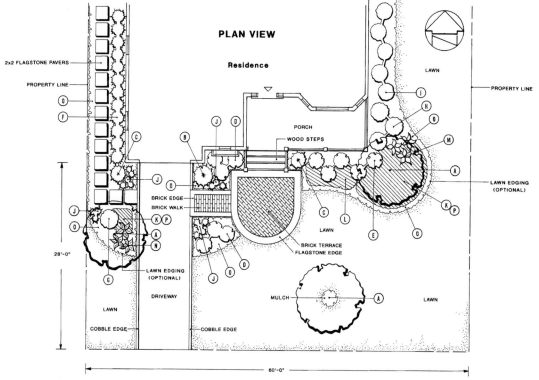

**PLAN VIEW**

Residence

2x2 FLAGSTONE PAVERS

PROPERTY LINE

Ⓞ
Ⓕ
Ⓒ
Ⓙ Ⓞ
Ⓙ Ⓞ
Ⓑ

PORCH
WOOD STEPS

BRICK EDGE
BRICK WALK

Ⓙ
Ⓞ
Ⓚ Ⓟ
Ⓐ
Ⓝ

LAWN EDGING
(OPTIONAL)

28'-0"

Ⓖ

DRIVEWAY

LAWN

COBBLE EDGE

Ⓙ
Ⓞ
Ⓓ

LAWN

BRICK TERRACE
FLAGSTONE EDGE

MULCH

COBBLE EDGE

LAWN

Ⓙ
Ⓗ
Ⓞ
Ⓜ
Ⓐ

LAWN EDGING
(OPTIONAL)

Ⓚ
Ⓟ

Ⓒ Ⓛ
Ⓔ Ⓞ

Ⓐ

PROPERTY LINE

60'-0"

## REGIONALIZED PLANT LISTS

Because climate and growing conditions vary greatly throughout North America, it is impossible to list here all the plants for this landscape plan that would do well everywhere on the continent. However, you can order a Blueprint Package with plant lists keyed to this plan and selected by expert horticulturists to thrive in your area.

The six-page Blueprint Package features a large-size version of this Plan View, plus a detailed regional Plant and Materials List. It also includes an illustrated list of hundreds of landscape plants suited to your region, in case you wish to make substitutions, as well as planting instructions and plant adaptation maps to ensure professional results with your new landscape.

See page 157 to order your regionalized Blueprint Package.

*The foundation border curving around the house provides the main source of interest in this landscape. However, maintaining it won't tax the easy-care gardener because the plants are compact and disease-resistant.*

# Rustic Tudor Home

"Charming" is the operative word for the landscape around this rustic stone-fronted house. The designer organizes the space into separate, easily maintained units that blend into a pleasing whole. The planting pockets—in front of the large window and the two areas bisected by pavers to the right of the drive—contain well-behaved plants that require little care to maintain their good looks. The small island of lawn can be quickly mowed, and maintenance is further reduced if lawn edging, which eliminates the need to edge by hand, is installed. A ribbon of small and moderate-sized shrubs, underplanted with a weed-smothering groundcover and spring bulbs, surrounds the lawn.

A single deciduous tree, set in a circle of bulbs and easy-care perennials that juts into the lawn, screens the entryway from street view and balances a triad of slow-growing, narrow conifers to the far left of the house. Shrubs in front of the windows were chosen for their low, unobtrusive growth habit. A dwarf conifer with pendulous branches forms the focal point of the shrub grouping in front of the larger window.

Paving is a strong unifying force in this design. The stone in the house facade is echoed in the walk that curves from the driveway up the steps to the landing and front door. Flagstone pavers border the other side of the drive and lead around the house. The cobblestone inlay at the foot of the drive not only breaks up the monotony of asphalt, but also visually carries the lawn border across the entire width of the property.

## Landscape Plan L284 shown in spring
*Designed by Salvatore A. Masullo*
Home Plan 2854
*For information about ordering blueprints for this home call 1-800-521-6797.*

**PLAN VIEW**

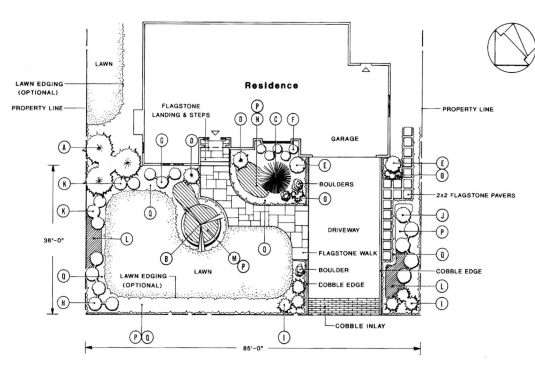

## REGIONALIZED PLANT LISTS

Because climate and growing conditions vary greatly throughout North America, it is impossible to list here all the plants for this landscape plan that would do well everywhere on the continent. However, you can order a Blueprint Package with plant lists keyed to this plan and selected by expert horticulturists to thrive in your area.

The six-page Blueprint Package features a large-size version of this Plan View, plus a detailed regional Plant and Materials List. It also includes an illustrated list of hundreds of landscape plants suited to your region, in case you wish to make substitutions, as well as planting instructions and plant adaptation maps to ensure professional results with your new landscape.

See page 157 to order your regionalized Blueprint Package.

*Although packed with interesting plants, this landscape is quite manageable for the easy-care gardener. Mowing the little island of lawn is a snap, and caring for the rest of the yard is just as easy, considering the shrubs don't need pruning and fall clean-up is minimal.*

*Lots of trees and large shrubs endow a suburban lot with the mood of a French country estate. To minimize pruning, the plants are carefully chosen for their upright shape, compact growth, and ability to stay within bounds over the years.*

## REGIONALIZED PLANT LISTS

Because climate and growing conditions vary greatly throughout North America, it is impossible to list here all the plants for this landscape plan that would do well everywhere on the continent. However, you can order a Blueprint Package with plant lists keyed to this plan and selected by expert horticulturists to thrive in your area.

The six-page Blueprint Package features a large-size version of this Plan View, plus a detailed regional Plant and Materials List. It also includes an illustrated list of hundreds of landscape plants suited to your region, in case you wish to make substitutions, as well as planting instructions and plant adaptation maps to ensure professional results with your new landscape.

See page 157 to order your regionalized Blueprint Package.

# French Country Home

An abundance of trees and shrubs surrounds this French country home, making it look more like a private, wooded estate in Europe rather than a suburban lot in New York, Iowa, or California. The flowering deciduous trees lined up along the front of the property are repeated near the entrance, leading your eye toward the front door. A single tree with an elegant weeping form and purple foliage provides an accent near the extension at the back of the house, and creates a focal point from the driveway entrance.

Some aspects of formality, while creating the grand look demanded by the architecture, are modified for ease of care. For instance, the dense, upright conifers set in a neat row along the driveway are allowed to grow naturally instead of being clipped into a formal hedge, which would require more labor. On the opposite side of the property, a staggered row of narrow conifers is also spaced for minimum pruning. The smooth expanse of green grass at the front of the lot gives the illusion that the house sits farther back than it really does, yet it is small enough to maintain without professional help.

A house this size needs plenty of parking space for family and friends. The designer breaks up the large expanse of driveway with decorative brick inlays and with a planting peninsula, which shields the garage from direct view. A parking bay near the front walk provides convenient parking for visitors, who can stroll right up the front walk toward the secluded entry courtyard after getting out of their cars.

## Landscape Plan L285 shown in spring
*Designed by Salvatore A. Masullo*
Home Plan 3559
*For information about ordering blueprints for this home call 1-800-521-6797.*

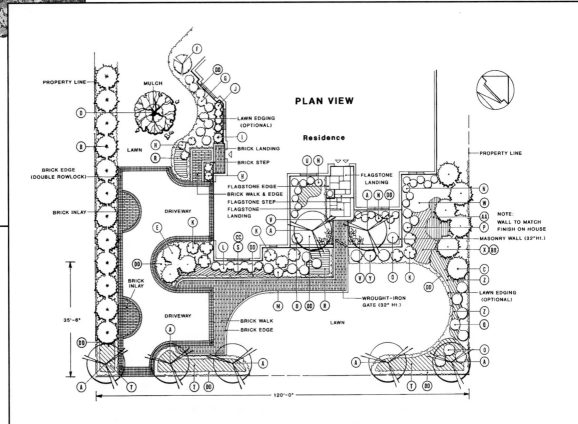

# Mediterranean-Style Home

Luxuriant mixed borders beautifully frame this large house, which is reminiscent of those in southern Europe. The borders impart a feeling of warmth and coziness to what might otherwise be an imposing structure. The distinct planting areas are arranged informally around the front walk, with its dramatic entry landings that angle from the driveway to the front porch. The various shrubs, ornamental grasses, groundcovers, perennials, and bulbs are chosen for colorful leaves or flowers and for textural interest. Because all these plants are compact or low-growing, they are easy to maintain and won't obscure the house's handsome detailing.

Even the deciduous trees anchoring the three major planting areas were selected for their compact, upright growth. They give the landscape needed height without shrouding the house. Balancing the triangle of trees is a larger deciduous tree in the strip of lawn next to the drive. This larger species, chosen for its slender shape and fine fall color, is set in a ring of mulch for easy mowing.

The paving materials are selected for durability and ease of care. A brick edging dresses up the concrete walk, and a cobblestone border adds interest to the asphalt driveway.

## Landscape Plan L286 shown in summer
*Designed by Damon Scott*
Home Plan 3602
*For information about ordering blueprints for this home call 1-800-521-6797.*

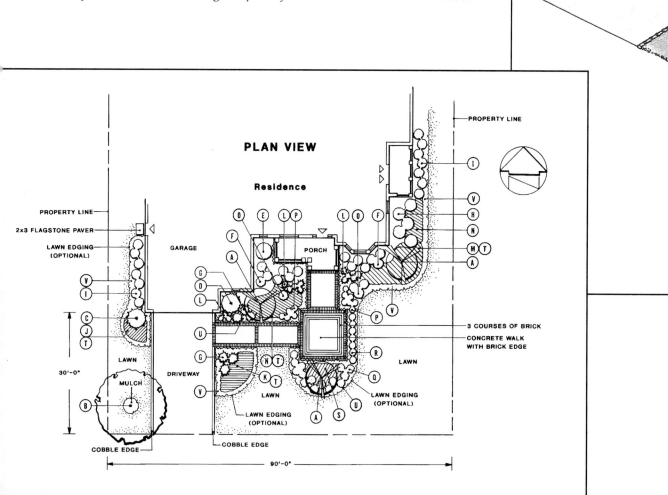

PLAN VIEW

Residence

PROPERTY LINE

PROPERTY LINE

2x3 FLAGSTONE PAVER

LAWN EDGING (OPTIONAL)

GARAGE

PORCH

3 COURSES OF BRICK

CONCRETE WALK WITH BRICK EDGE

LAWN

LAWN EDGING (OPTIONAL)

30'-0"

LAWN

MULCH

DRIVEWAY

LAWN

LAWN EDGING (OPTIONAL)

COBBLE EDGE

COBBLE EDGE

90'-0"

## REGIONALIZED PLANT LISTS

Because climate and growing conditions vary greatly throughout North America, it is impossible to list here all the plants for this landscape plan that would do well everywhere on the continent. However, you can order a Blueprint Package with plant lists keyed to this plan and selected by expert horticulturists to thrive in your area.

The six-page Blueprint Package features a large-size version of this Plan View, plus a detailed regional Plant and Materials List. It also includes an illustrated list of hundreds of landscape plants suited to your region, in case you wish to make substitutions, as well as planting instructions and plant adaptation maps to ensure professional results with your new landscape.

See page 157 to order your regionalized Blueprint Package.

*A sequence of long-blooming perennials, combined with shrubs and groundcovers that feature purple-bronze foliage, creates a colorful setting for this dramatic home.*

*All the trees in this landscape grow in beds and borders filled with groundcovers. The groundcovers smother weeds, absorb fallen leaves, and keep trees healthy by protecting them from mower nicks.*

## REGIONALIZED PLANT LISTS

Because climate and growing conditions vary greatly throughout North America, it is impossible to list here all the plants for this landscape plan that would do well everywhere on the continent. However, you can order a Blueprint Package with plant lists keyed to this plan and selected by expert horticulturists to thrive in your area.

The six-page Blueprint Package features a large-size version of this Plan View, plus a detailed regional Plant and Materials List. It also includes an illustrated list of hundreds of landscape plants suited to your region, in case you wish to make substitutions, as well as planting instructions and plant adaptation maps to ensure professional results with your new landscape.

See page 157 to order your regionalized Blueprint Package.

# European-Flair Home

The designer uses graceful curving borders, stepped back to mimic the jogs in the large European-style home, to bring this landscape to life. An appealing mix of shrubs grown for their ornamental foliage, flowers, and fruit rises from an underplanting of weed-smothering groundcovers and long-blooming perennials. The shrubs' compact growth habits keep the windows clear and save on pruning chores. A small tree, selected for its handsome branching pattern and long season of colorful foliage, partially screens the entry from public view and creates a dramatic focal point.

The curves in the borders are repeated in the cobble-edged planting peninsulas, which visually break up the large expanse of asphalt in the drive. Five deciduous shade trees planted along the drive spruce up this utilitarian area while giving needed height to the landscape. The trees are chosen for their airy canopies of delicate leaves, which create a softening screen without excessive shade or fall cleanup.

A flagstone walk, set in concrete and mortared for weed-free maintenance, zigzags from the drive to the front porch. For a greater feeling of privacy, the designer ends the walk short of the street so that it is accessible only from the drive.

The curving borders jut into the lawn, giving it an appealing shape—and a size that isn't too large for the easy-care gardener to handle comfortably. The lawn is kept free of plantings and other obstacles to make mowing faster and easier.

## Landscape Plan L287 shown in spring

*Designed by Edward D. Georges*
Home Plan 3558
*For information about ordering blueprints for this home call 1-800-521-6797.*

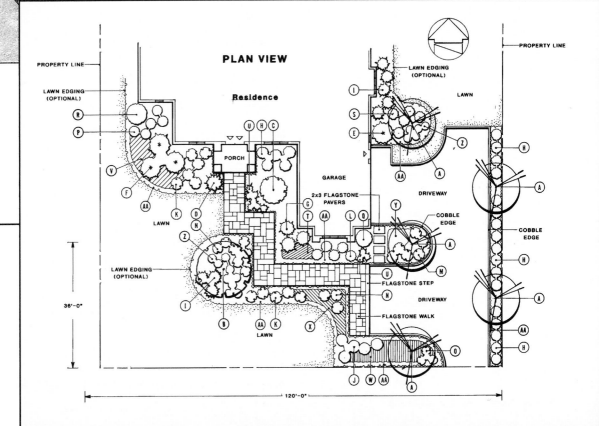

PLAN VIEW

PROPERTY LINE

LAWN EDGING (OPTIONAL)

Residence

PROPERTY LINE

LAWN EDGING (OPTIONAL)

LAWN

PORCH

GARAGE

2x3 FLAGSTONE PAVERS

DRIVEWAY

COBBLE EDGE

COBBLE EDGE

LAWN

LAWN EDGING (OPTIONAL)

FLAGSTONE STEP

DRIVEWAY

FLAGSTONE WALK

LAWN

36'-0"

120'-0"

*Brick is the main unifying element in this charming landscape, giving the design a sense of serenity. Brick also serves a practical purpose, by keeping plants in bounds and reducing lawn-edging chores.*

## REGIONALIZED PLANT LISTS

Because climate and growing conditions vary greatly throughout North America, it is impossible to list here all the plants for this landscape plan that would do well everywhere on the continent. However, you can order a Blueprint Package with plant lists keyed to this plan and selected by expert horticulturists to thrive in your area.

The six-page Blueprint Package features a large-size version of this Plan View, plus a detailed regional Plant and Materials List. It also includes an illustrated list of hundreds of landscape plants suited to your region, in case you wish to make substitutions, as well as planting instructions and plant adaptation maps to ensure professional results with your new landscape.

See page 157 to order your regionalized Blueprint Package.

# Traditional Two-Story Home

T he designer includes brick features throughout this design—in the walkways, mowing strip, driveway edging, decorative low wall, and lamp piers—to visually link the landscape to the brick-facade home. This creates a sense of serenity and unity. Set in concrete and mortared for easy upkeep, the brick elements add warmth and color to the scene and help keep plantings neatly in place.

Also serving as a unifying element and providing year-round appeal is the trio of handsome multi-trunked specimen trees, with their colorful flaking bark. The foundation plantings consist of attractive low-growing and dwarf shrubs underplanted with groundcovers, perennials, and bulbs. Foliage plants chosen for their good looks are combined with flowering and fruiting plants for a long season of interest. Extended along the property lines, the mixed plantings contrast beautifully with the brick edgings. The right-angled brick wall in front of the entry creates a sense of enclosure and forms the backdrop for a spring bulb show.

The irregularly shaped lawn in front of the wall and its accompanying patch next to the drive are relatively small and won't overburden the gardener who wants to limit maintenance chores. The mower wheels can rest on the brick mowing strip, making lawn mowing and edging a breeze.

## Landscape Plan L288 shown in spring

*Designed by Salvatore A. Masullo*
Home Plan 3452
*For information about ordering blueprints for this home call 1-800-521-6797.*

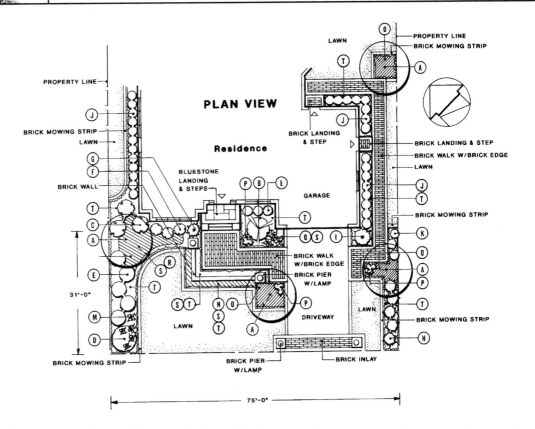

*Although heavily wooded, this landscape is easy to maintain because the trees and shrubs are well-behaved and won't outgrow their allotted space. The underplantings absorb most of the leaves from the deciduous trees, which put on a flaming show of color in fall.*

### REGIONALIZED PLANT LISTS

Because climate and growing conditions vary greatly throughout North America, it is impossible to list here all the plants for this landscape plan that would do well everywhere on the continent. However, you can order a Blueprint Package with plant lists keyed to this plan and selected by expert horticulturists to thrive in your area.

The six-page Blueprint Package features a large-size version of this Plan View, plus a detailed regional Plant and Materials List. It also includes an illustrated list of hundreds of landscape plants suited to your region, in case you wish to make substitutions, as well as planting instructions and plant adaptation maps to ensure professional results with your new landscape.

See page 157 to order your regionalized Blueprint Package.

# Volume-Look Home

This irregularly shaped sprawling home, which sits on a large lot, gets a comfortable sense of seclusion from its extensive plantings of trees and shrubs. The designer includes plenty of evergreens so that fall leaf clean-up isn't a burdensome task. Clusters of conifers, both screening trees and attractive dwarf forms, appear at the edges of the landscape. Broadleaved evergreens in the borders and foundation plantings are selected for their high-gloss leaves and compact growth.

The designer chooses an elegant white floral scheme to complement the largely green landscape. Seven deciduous trees lining the curving drive provide a spectacular flower show early in the season. A specimen tree and an adjoining trio of small flowering trees to the left of the property near the house contribute spectacular spring blossoms as well as handsome branching habits. The trees are underplanted with white-flowering shrubs, perennials, and bulbs in a weed-smothering blanket of evergreen groundcover.

A generous amount of brick paving ties the landscape to the brick-facade house. Brick pavers appear in the walks, along and across the top of the drive, and in the decorative planters near the front door. The only annuals in the design are grown in the planters, where they can be easily watered.

A sweeping oval of lawn on the left side of the lot is partially hidden by trees, while an irregular patch on the right side is exposed. Devoid of obstacles that would slow down a mower, the lawn areas can be tended fairly quickly by the homeowner.

## Landscape Plan L289 shown in spring
*Designed by Jim Morgan*
Home Plan 3310
*For information about ordering blueprints for this home call 1-800-521-6797.*

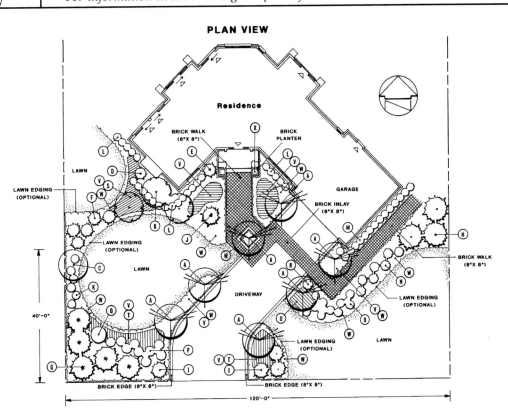

**PLAN VIEW**

Residence

BRICK WALK (8"X 8")

BRICK PLANTER

GARAGE

BRICK INLAY (8"X 8")

LAWN

LAWN EDGING (OPTIONAL)

LAWN EDGING (OPTIONAL)

LAWN

DRIVEWAY

BRICK WALK (8"X 8")

LAWN EDGING (OPTIONAL)

LAWN

LAWN EDGING (OPTIONAL)

40'-0"

BRICK EDGE (8"X 8")

BRICK EDGE (8"X 8")

120'-0"

# Traditional One-Story Home

This classic house style, with its steep roofline and tidy clapboards, demands a traditional, shade-tree-filled landscape. Fulfilling that function is a trio of elegantly branching deciduous trees. A specimen tree in the foundation planting on the left of the house provides dramatic spring blossoms and summer shade.

The trees and shrubs in the beds are underplanted with groundcovers, perennials, and bulbs. All the plants in the design are chosen for ease of care and for their attractive foliage, flowers, or fruit. For instance, the clusters of tough bronze-leaved shrubs flanking the foot of the drive provide eye-catching color most of the year and remain low enough so they won't block a driver's view. The foundation plantings contain compact plants that won't block the windows or the decorative wooden porch railing. The planting pocket marking the front walk holds low plants that won't engulf the lamppost or obscure light from the lamp.

The designer chooses flagstones and cobblestones to complement the home's traditional clapboards. Flagstones in the walk and on the porch landing are mortared for weed-free upkeep, while the pavers leading around the garage are set in groundcover. The cobble inlay visually extends the plantings across the drive, and the edging serves as a mowing strip. The patches of lawn on both sides of the drive are designed for fast mowing. The ring of mulch under the tree protects the trunk and eliminates the need to hand trim.

## Landscape Plan L290 shown in spring

*Designed by Jeffrey Diefenbach*
Home Plan 2947
*For information about ordering blueprints for this home call 1-800-521-6797.*

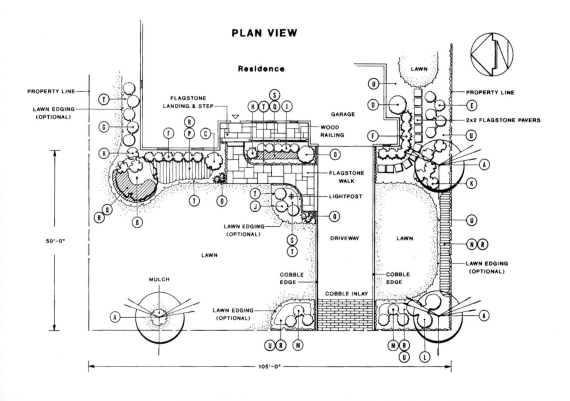

PLAN VIEW

Residence

PROPERTY LINE
LAWN EDGING (OPTIONAL)
FLAGSTONE LANDING & STEP
GARAGE
WOOD RAILING
LAWN
PROPERTY LINE
2x2 FLAGSTONE PAVERS
FLAGSTONE WALK
LIGHTPOST
LAWN EDGING (OPTIONAL)
DRIVEWAY
LAWN
LAWN EDGING (OPTIONAL)
LAWN
MULCH
COBBLE EDGE
COBBLE EDGE
LAWN EDGING (OPTIONAL)
COBBLE INLAY
50'-0"
105'-0"

## REGIONALIZED PLANT LISTS

Because climate and growing conditions vary greatly throughout North America, it is impossible to list here all the plants for this landscape plan that would do well everywhere on the continent. However, you can order a Blueprint Package with plant lists keyed to this plan and selected by expert horticulturists to thrive in your area.

The six-page Blueprint Package features a large-size version of this Plan View, plus a detailed regional Plant and Materials List. It also includes an illustrated list of hundreds of landscape plants suited to your region, in case you wish to make substitutions, as well as planting instructions and plant adaptation maps to ensure professional results with your new landscape.

See page 157 to order your regionalized Blueprint Package.

*This easy-care landscape contains graceful shade trees, compact shrubs, and an assortment of colorful perennials and bulbs. Weed-free flagstones and cobblestones complement the home's wood siding.*

# Early American One-Story

The designer cleverly employs stone, the dominant feature of Early American homes like this one, to unify the landscape and create a snug entry court. The flagstone-capped stone walls forming the courtyard make a handsome backdrop for a variety of compact evergreen shrubs—some chosen for colorful fruit, others for bright blue-gray needles or glossy green leaves.

A cobblestone edging beautifies the driveway and leads to an inlaid rectangle of cobbles that serves as a gateway to the courtyard. Inside the court, an inlaid flagstone arch points the way to the front door. Mortared flagstone continues up the steps and onto the landing, while in the side yard individual square flagstone pavers rest in a low groundcover.

Reinforcing the sense of privacy created by the courtyard is a threesome of large trees, chosen for their fine upward-sweeping canopies and fiery fall foliage. For ease of care, each tree is underplanted with leaf-absorbing groundcovers, long-blooming perennials, and spring bulbs. The designer selects a small specimen tree on the right side of the lot near the house for its seasonal blossoms, great fall color, and attractive branching pattern.

## Landscape Plan L291 shown in spring

*Designed by Jeffrey Diefenbach*
Home Plan 2916
*For information about ordering blueprints for this home call 1-800-521-6797.*

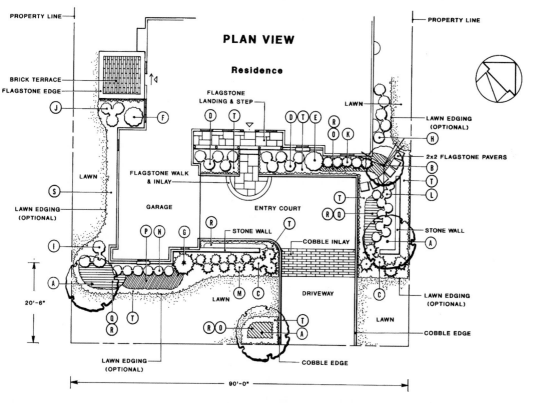

**PLAN VIEW**

Residence

PROPERTY LINE

PROPERTY LINE

BRICK TERRACE
FLAGSTONE EDGE

FLAGSTONE
LANDING & STEP

LAWN

LAWN EDGING
(OPTIONAL)

2x2 FLAGSTONE PAVERS

LAWN

FLAGSTONE WALK
& INLAY

STONE WALL

LAWN EDGING
(OPTIONAL)

GARAGE

ENTRY COURT

STONE WALL

COBBLE INLAY

LAWN EDGING
(OPTIONAL)

LAWN

DRIVEWAY

LAWN EDGING
(OPTIONAL)

20'-6"

LAWN

COBBLE EDGE

LAWN EDGING
(OPTIONAL)

COBBLE EDGE

90'-0"

## REGIONALIZED PLANT LISTS

Because climate and growing conditions vary greatly throughout North America, it is impossible to list here all the plants for this landscape plan that would do well everywhere on the continent. However, you can order a Blueprint Package with plant lists keyed to this plan and selected by expert horticulturists to thrive in your area.

The six-page Blueprint Package features a large-size version of this Plan View, plus a detailed regional Plant and Materials List. It also includes an illustrated list of hundreds of landscape plants suited to your region, in case you wish to make substitutions, as well as planting instructions and plant adaptation maps to ensure professional results with your new landscape.

See page 157 to order your regionalized Blueprint Package.

*Low-growing shrubs, which won't need pruning to keep them from obscuring the house and stone wall, are important features in this easy-care design.*

*Repetition of forms, curves, and paving unifies the landscape design for this traditional New England-style home.*

## REGIONALIZED PLANT LISTS

Because climate and growing conditions vary greatly throughout North America, it is impossible to list here all the plants for this landscape plan that would do well everywhere on the continent. However, you can order a Blueprint Package with plant lists keyed to this plan and selected by expert horticulturists to thrive in your area.

The six-page Blueprint Package features a large-size version of this Plan View, plus a detailed regional Plant and Materials List. It also includes an illustrated list of hundreds of landscape plants suited to your region, in case you wish to make substitutions, as well as planting instructions and plant adaptation maps to ensure professional results with your new landscape.

See page 157 to order your regionalized Blueprint Package.

# Cape Cod Traditional

The quaint character of this traditional Cape Cod home calls for an intimate, comfortable landscape that reflects the formality of the house without being stiff or unfriendly. Notice how the repetition of curves throughout the landscape works to unite the design into a cohesive whole. The clean, curving line of the large shrub border, which sweeps directly from the foundation planting toward the street, is repeated in the smaller curves of the planting borders along the street and in the shapes of the lawn areas. The stone walk and the driveway feature flowing curves. The front walk attractively leads to both the driveway and the street, where guests will probably park their cars.

Loose, informally shaped trees soften the lines of the house and complement the curves of the landscape. By positioning these trees at the front edge of the property and in the center of the walkway, the designer buffers the view of the house from the street, creating a sense of privacy while framing the home. Evergreen foundation shrubs used near the house match the traditional style of the architecture. Elsewhere, flowering shrubs provide seasonal color.

This landscape design works successfully because the gentle, repetitive lines and forms, which remain apparent even in the winter, unify the property, making it seem larger than it is.

## Landscape Plan L200 shown in spring
*Designed by James Morgan*
Home Plan 2657
*For information about ordering blueprints for this home call 1-800-521-6797.*

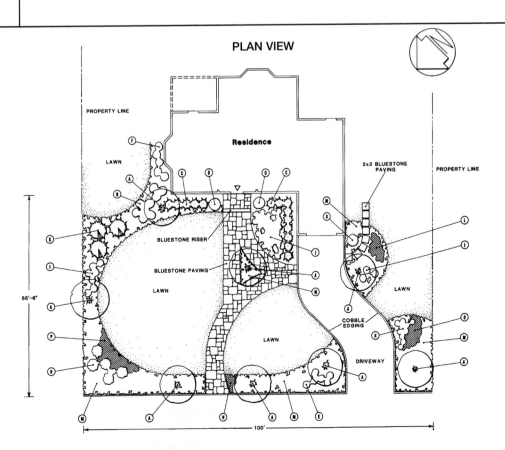

**PLAN VIEW**

PROPERTY LINE

LAWN

Residence

2x2 BLUESTONE PAVING

PROPERTY LINE

BLUESTONE RISER

BLUESTONE PAVING

LAWN

LAWN

LAWN

COBBLE EDGING

DRIVEWAY

55'-6"

100'

*Highlighted by a pleasing front walk that incorporates several turns, a change in levels, and a charming white picket fence, the landscape design for this small property effectively transforms the house into a picture-perfect cottage.*

## REGIONALIZED PLANT LISTS

Because climate and growing conditions vary greatly throughout North America, it is impossible to list here all the plants for this landscape plan that would do well everywhere on the continent. However, you can order a Blueprint Package with plant lists keyed to this plan and selected by expert horticulturists to thrive in your area.

The six-page Blueprint Package features a large-size version of this Plan View, plus a detailed regional Plant and Materials List. It also includes an illustrated list of hundreds of landscape plants suited to your region, in case you wish to make substitutions, as well as planting instructions and plant adaptation maps to ensure professional results with your new landscape.

See page 157 to order your regionalized Blueprint Package.

# Cape Cod Cottage

S killful landscaping transforms this small Cape Cod house into a cozy, quaint cottage that has instant curb appeal. Relying on an exuberant mix of flowering shrubs and perennials, the design evokes the mood of a friendly country home whose bountiful gardens burst with colorful flowers.

Notice how the designer links the front walk to the driveway with a few pleasing turns and a change of levels, rather than dissecting the small property with a front walk leading straight to the street. This layout adds visual interest to the small yard while making it seem broader. The white picket fence not only adds to the cottage-garden charm, but also gives the landscape some depth and a feeling of intimacy.

Massed together into several large planting beds, graceful trees, flowering shrubs, groundcovers, and perennials border the house and entryway to create an ever-changing informal garden setting. Small boulders add a naturalistic character reminiscent of New England, and also provide a year-round structure to the beds. Planted along the base of the fence, perennials add color during the summer and soften the fence without hiding it. A deciduous shrub with strong spring color highlights the corner of the fenced garden, while evergreen flowering specimens brighten the corners of the house.

To balance the weight of the entry bed and paving, the designer places a small tree and planting bed at the front corner of the driveway. These plants provide a colorful greeting as guests and family members approach the house.

## Landscape Plan L202 shown in spring
*Designed by Michael J. Opisso*
Home Plan 2661
*For information about ordering blueprints for this home call 1-800-521-6797.*

**PLAN VIEW**

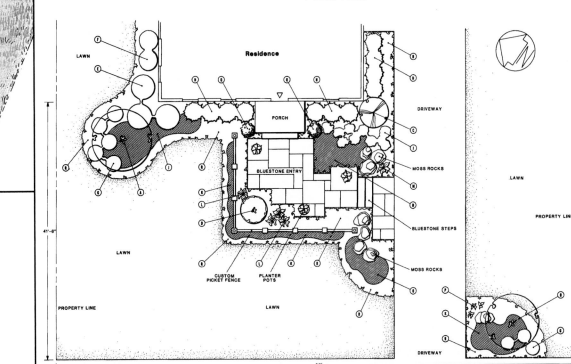

# Front-Porch Farmhouse

This home's cozy covered porch makes a comfortable place to relax in summer and enjoy the evening air. For that reason, the designers choose plenty of summer-blooming plants with white flowers, which shine in the moonlight after other colors in the garden have faded from view.

Although fairly small, the front yard contains a lively assortment of native plants chosen for their year-round interest and ease of care. Suited to the climate and growing conditions, they do well without much maintenance. Lawn upkeep is minimal because the patches are small and shaped for quick, efficient mowing.

At first glance, the identical pools of lawn and the repeated plantings on either side of the walk give a strong impression of symmetry, but the designers soften the look with the irregular arrangement of flagstones and by varying the other plantings from side to side. For example, a tree by the left porch corner balances a planting of perennials and shrubs at the opposite corner.

The front walk leads conveniently from the street parking and sidewalk to the home's entrance. Access from the driveway is from an inconspicuous walkway that leads to the porch's side steps near the mudroom entrance.

## Landscape Plan L292 shown in summer

*Designed by Maria Morrison and Damon Scott*
Home Plan 3396
*For information about ordering blueprints for this home call 1-800-521-6797.*

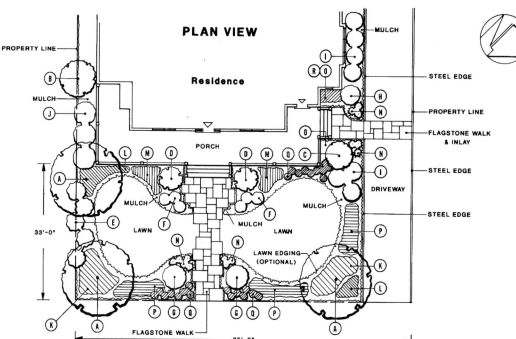

## REGIONALIZED PLANT LISTS

Because climate and growing conditions vary greatly throughout North America, it is impossible to list here all the plants for this landscape plan that would do well everywhere on the continent. However, you can order a Blueprint Package with plant lists keyed to this plan and selected by expert horticulturists to thrive in your area.

The six-page Blueprint Package features a large-size version of this Plan View, plus a detailed regional Plant and Materials List. It also includes an illustrated list of hundreds of landscape plants suited to your region, in case you wish to make substitutions, as well as planting instructions and plant adaptation maps to ensure professional results with your new landscape.

See page 157 to order your regionalized Blueprint Package.

*The snug porch is a restful place from which to enjoy the diversity of native plants that fill this small, easy-care front yard.*

# Contemporary Farmhouse

S ome landscapes shine in one season and then retreat into boring greenery for the rest of the growing season—but not this one! It features a triad of handsome trees whose foliage emerges bright purple-red in spring, matures to deep burgundy-purple, and then changes to red in autumn. The specimen tree, shrubs, bulbs, perennials, and ornamental grasses bloom in sequence from spring through fall, so there is always something happening in this front yard.

The designer selects the plants not just for their colorful attributes but also for their restrained habits, making maintenance manageable for easy-care gardeners. To reduce upkeep further, screen plantings are arranged informally so that the shrubs grow naturally without pruning, and deciduous plants are situated so that fallen leaves filter mainly into groundcovers. Even lawn mowing is simple, since there are no corners to turn—pushing the mower in a spiral polishes off the job quickly.

Brick edging and a generous landing break up the long stretch of asphalt and tie the driveway to the landscape, while creating a space for passengers to exit from their cars. The brick inlay and edging lead into a U-shaped walk that cuts through the upper curve of the lawn and forms a separate planting area filled with decorative plants. The brick walk leads to the flagstone terrace set beneath the roof overhang and the home's front entrance, while two flagstones through the border provide a shortcut to on-street parking.

## Landscape Plan L293 shown in summer
*Designed by Edward D. Georges*
Home Plan 3438
*For information about ordering blueprints for this home call 1-800-521-6797.*

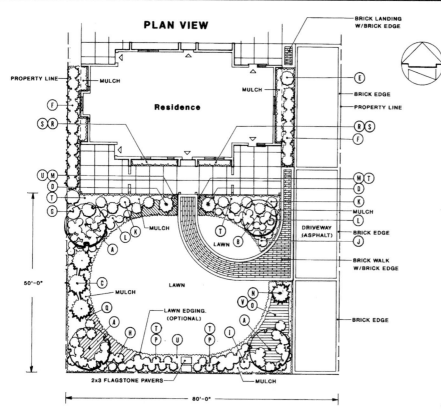

## REGIONALIZED PLANT LISTS

Because climate and growing conditions vary greatly throughout North America, it is impossible to list here all the plants for this landscape plan that would do well everywhere on the continent. However, you can order a Blueprint Package with plant lists keyed to this plan and selected by expert horticulturists to thrive in your area.

The six-page Blueprint Package features a large-size version of this Plan View, plus a detailed regional Plant and Materials List. It also includes an illustrated list of hundreds of landscape plants suited to your region, in case you wish to make substitutions, as well as planting instructions and plant adaptation maps to ensure professional results with your new landscape.

See page 157 to order your regionalized Blueprint Package.

*The strong curving lines of this design's lawn and walkway make a pleasing contrast to the home's angles, while echoing the dramatic curved window over the front entrance.*

*The designer shapes the lawn in a truncated S to create a graceful curve that offsets the angles in the architecture. Seasonal color comes from the sequence of bloom of easy-care shrubs, groundcovers, perennials, and bulbs.*

## REGIONALIZED PLANT LISTS

Because climate and growing conditions vary greatly throughout North America, it is impossible to list here all the plants for this landscape plan that would do well everywhere on the continent. However, you can order a Blueprint Package with plant lists keyed to this plan and selected by expert horticulturists to thrive in your area.

The six-page Blueprint Package features a large-size version of this Plan View, plus a detailed regional Plant and Materials List. It also includes an illustrated list of hundreds of landscape plants suited to your region, in case you wish to make substitutions, as well as planting instructions and plant adaptation maps to ensure professional results with your new landscape.

See page 157 to order your regionalized Blueprint Package.

# Wood-Sided Contemporary

Five deciduous trees scattered in this relatively small front yard give the property a woodsy feeling. At the same time, they soften the house's sharp lines, creating privacy and light shade. The designer chooses the trees to create an attractive association of rounded and upright forms, and for their moderate growth, handsome branching patterns, and tidy, easy-to-clean-up-after leaves.

The two lawn areas are small enough for easy upkeep, which is made even easier if the optional lawn edging is installed. The patch in front of the house is laid out in an appealing S-shaped curve. Low-growing shrubs at the top of the curve remain naturally below window level without pruning. Shrubs on the left side of the property and to the right of the garage are arranged in informal hedges that don't require clipping. An assortment of easy-care spring bulbs and long-blooming perennials provide a sequence of bloom from spring through fall.

Instead of creating a straight path to the entry, the designer interrupts the flow of the flagstone walk with planting areas that jut into the sides, to give it more interest and soften the long wall. Potted annuals and an espaliered shrub trained on a trellis provide additional appeal on the way to the front landing.

## Landscape Plan L294 shown in spring

*Designed by Jeffrey Diefenbach*
Home Plan 2822
*For information about ordering blueprints for this home call 1-800-521-6797.*

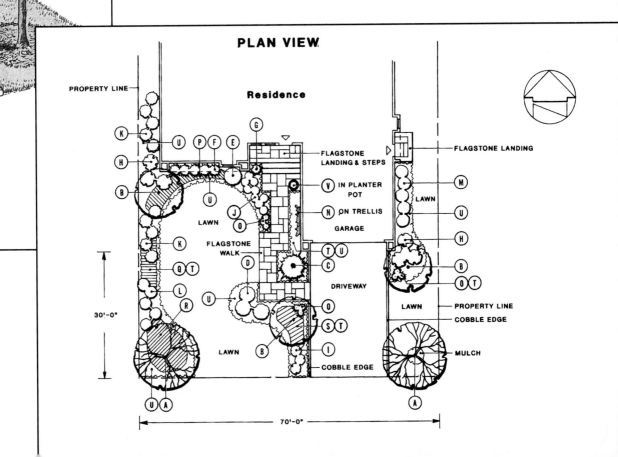

**PLAN VIEW**

PROPERTY LINE

Residence

FLAGSTONE LANDING & STEPS

FLAGSTONE LANDING

V IN PLANTER POT

N ON TRELLIS

GARAGE

LAWN

LAWN

FLAGSTONE WALK

DRIVEWAY

LAWN

PROPERTY LINE

COBBLE EDGE

MULCH

LAWN

COBBLE EDGE

30'-0"

70'-0"

# View-Lot Contemporary

The designer of this attractive, leafy landscape eschews lawn in favor of undemanding groundcovers and paving materials, allowing the home-owners to keep their mower in deep storage! The yard needs no regular upkeep, so is perfect for folks who travel a lot or who don't have the time or energy for yard care.

The designer uses both curving shapes and straight lines in the design to create variety of form. Small graveled areas surrounded by groundcover—one features an artistic arrangement of moss rocks—replace what might have been the lawn in a more traditional landscape. The brick walk leads to a wooden deck that doubles as a dramatic entry court, creating a beautiful, easy-care entrance. The brick walk's strong geometric lines balance the curves in the landscape, and its reddish hue adds warmth to the wood decking and gravel pools.

The deciduous trees are selected for their small, delicate foliage, which can be cleaned from the hardscape and gravel with a leaf blower every autumn. Other plantings include flowering perennials that aren't fussy, ornamental grasses that require only a haircut once a year in late winter, and small-scale shrubs that don't need pruning. Chosen for their subdued growth, the groundcovers require edging once a year to keep their crisp outlines. Land-scape fabric lies beneath the gravel to prevent weeds from poking through.

## Landscape Plan L295 shown in autumn

*Designed by Michael J. Opisso*
Home Plan 2937
*For information about ordering blueprints for this home call 1-800-521-6797.*

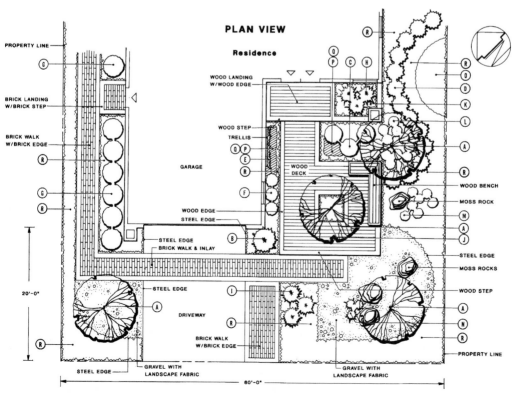

**PLAN VIEW**

Residence

PROPERTY LINE

WOOD LANDING W/WOOD EDGE

BRICK LANDING W/BRICK STEP

WOOD STEP
TRELLIS

BRICK WALK W/BRICK EDGE

GARAGE

WOOD DECK

WOOD BENCH

MOSS ROCK

WOOD EDGE
STEEL EDGE

STEEL EDGE
BRICK WALK & INLAY

STEEL EDGE
MOSS ROCKS

STEEL EDGE

WOOD STEP

20'-0"

DRIVEWAY

BRICK WALK W/BRICK EDGE

PROPERTY LINE

STEEL EDGE

GRAVEL WITH LANDSCAPE FABRIC

GRAVEL WITH LANDSCAPE FABRIC

60'-0"

## REGIONALIZED PLANT LISTS

Because climate and growing conditions vary greatly throughout North America, it is impossible to list here all the plants for this landscape plan that would do well everywhere on the continent. However, you can order a Blueprint Package with plant lists keyed to this plan and selected by expert horticulturists to thrive in your area.

The six-page Blueprint Package features a large-size version of this Plan View, plus a detailed regional Plant and Materials List. It also includes an illustrated list of hundreds of landscape plants suited to your region, in case you wish to make substitutions, as well as planting instructions and plant adaptation maps to ensure professional results with your new landscape.

See page 157 to order your regionalized Blueprint Package.

*Maintaining this lawnless front yard is a snap: Cut back the perennials in late winter, edge the groundcovers once a year in early summer, and clean up with a leaf blower once or twice in fall.*

# CHAPTER 4

# Easy-Care Backyards

*These Carefree Landscape Designs Suit
Every Situation and Appeal to Every Taste*

Design: Tom Pellett

The following pages offer irrefutable proof that well-designed backyard landscapes can be both beautiful and functional without requiring a lot of upkeep! The secret is to rely on colorful, undemanding, well-behaved plants and easy-to-maintain hardscape, and to combine them in a pleasing way. Luckily, you don't have to study garden design or develop an artistic eye if you haven't already done so. Our professional landscape designers have done the work for you, creating 23 backyard landscapes to suit a wide range of situations and preferences. In their skilled hands, a low-maintenance landscape is anything but dull and unimaginative.

As you look over the designs, you'll see that you can have the type of landscape you've always wanted without having to spend too much time tending it. Whether you want a place to throw parties or just a pretty spot for loafing or swimming, you'll find it here. If you'd like lots of wildflowers, a yard full of birds, or enduring fragrance, look no further than these pages. If you want to expand your living space or simply enjoy nature, you'll find plenty of low-maintenance options.

The plans include choices for sunny sites as well as shady ones, so if you have a heavily treed lot, you won't have to give up the shade to have a beautiful garden. Most of the plans feature small, easy-to-care-for lawns, but there are lawnless designs for those who don't want to perform any weekly chores at all. Some of the plans feature easy-care native plants and wildflowers, while others include selections from around the world. However, in both cases, if you decide to order a plan, only those plants that grow well in your region will be included in the plant list that accompanies the detailed blueprints.

If you don't need an entire landscape, then consider getting plans for one of the borders, which are designed to run the length of one side of an average-sized lot. You can choose an easy-care English-style flower border; a border designed for a shady site; a mixed border of shrubs, groundcovers, and flowers; or one that relies mainly on shrubs for low-maintenance and privacy.

A shady backyard becomes a dreamy naturalistic setting when planted
with layers of plants. An understory of small trees and shrubs gives dimension
to the scene, while a carpet of wildflowers and shade-loving foliage plants
creates intimacy.

# Shade-Filled Refuge

This design demonstrates that it's entirely possible to have your shade trees and your garden, too. Existing mature trees that cast a lot of shade need not deter you from having a beautiful flower-filled yard, as long as the trees aren't shallow-rooted. The trick lies in eliminating the lawn, which struggles in low light, and replacing it with hardscape and shade-tolerant plantings. The designer chooses flowering shrubs that thrive in the shade to give the space year-round structure and color, and then fills in with an assortment of shade-loving flowers and ferns.

Every inch of this shady yard is designed for beauty and outdoor living. An irregularly shaped walk and patio mirroring the lines of the house lead to an octagonal seating area ideal for dining, chatting, or playing games. For a more private retreat, you can follow the stepping stones to the gazebo. For a closer look at the flowers, you can stroll along the circular path from the seating area.

A thick mulch covers the garden floor—an essential work-saving feature, since mulch discourages weeds and keeps the soil cool and moist. Although a lot of plants are specified in the design, most are undemanding. An informal effect is the goal, so compulsive tidying is not necessary to keep the landscape looking good. The only regular maintenance you'll need to perform is to water weekly during rainless summer weather and to sweep the patio and walk occasionally. Autumn and late winter chores include a weekend spent raking leaves and cutting back the dead tops of the perennials.

## Landscape Plan L296 shown in spring
*Designed by Jeffrey Diefenbach*
For Gazebo Plan JJG215, see page 149

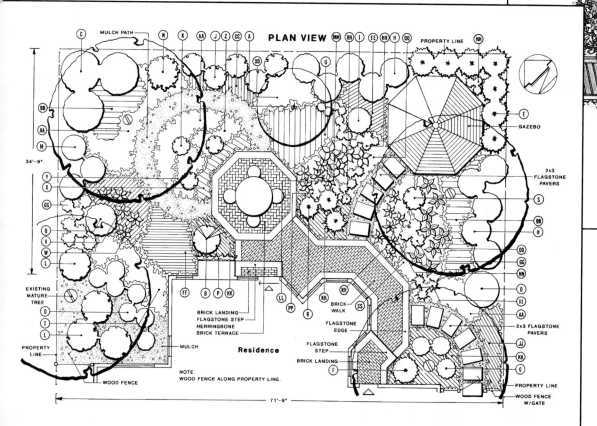

## REGIONALIZED PLANT LISTS

Because climate and growing conditions vary greatly throughout North America, it is impossible to list here all the plants for this landscape plan that would do well everywhere on the continent. However, you can order a Blueprint Package with plant lists keyed to this plan and selected by expert horticulturists to thrive in your area.

The six-page Blueprint Package features a large-size version of this Plan View, plus a detailed regional Plant and Materials List. It also includes an illustrated list of hundreds of landscape plants suited to your region, in case you wish to make substitutions, as well as planting instructions and plant adaptation maps to ensure professional results with your new landscape.

See page 157 to order your regionalized Blueprint Package.

*Mature shade trees need not be a deterrent to a flower-filled backyard. This shady landscape is built around four existing mature shade trees, but can be easily adjusted for a different number of trees or trees in different locations.*

*Wildflowers and native shrubs turn a shady, tree-filled site into an easy-care paradise. Because there is no lawn, weekly maintenance chores are practically non-existent.*

## REGIONALIZED PLANT LISTS

Because climate and growing conditions vary greatly throughout North America, it is impossible to list here all the plants for this landscape plan that would do well everywhere on the continent. However, you can order a Blueprint Package with plant lists keyed to this plan and selected by expert horticulturists to thrive in your area.

The six-page Blueprint Package features a large-size version of this Plan View, plus a detailed regional Plant and Materials List. It also includes an illustrated list of hundreds of landscape plants suited to your region, in case you wish to make substitutions, as well as planting instructions and plant adaptation maps to ensure professional results with your new landscape.

See page 157 to order your regionalized Blueprint Package.

# Native Shade Garden

Take advantage of existing mature trees already gracing your yard to create a woodland garden filled with colorful native shrubs, perennial wildflowers, and ferns. Because plants that grow naturally in a region require less work, this design is not only beautiful and ecological, it's practical, too!

Many woodland wildflowers die to the ground in mid-summer after putting on a flowery spring show, so the designer carefully sites longer-lasting and evergreen types near the patio and house to provide summer-long color, and uses the ephemerals (those that die to the ground in summer) where they won't be missed later in the year. The garden includes native flowering shrubs to provide structure, form, flowers, and foliage through the changing seasons.

In addition to permanent woody plants, sizable areas of paving contribute to the garden's strong structure and low maintenance. The flagstones in the walk and circular terrace are arranged informally, in keeping with the garden's casual style. The pool of gravel substitutes for lawn (turf struggles in such a shady site) and is underlaid with landscape fabric to thwart weeds and reduce maintenance. The lack of lawn makes weekly chores almost nonexistent.

The low stone wall flanked by boulders echoes the terrace's curve and visually separates the plantings behind it, making the yard seem more expansive. Flagstone pavers lead from the terrace to the gravel pool and past a charming roofed garden swing. Set at the yard's perimeter, the structure offers a relaxing spot for solitary contemplation or a tête-a-tête.

## Landscape Plan L298 shown in spring
*Designed by Damon Scott*
For Garden Swing Plan, see page 147

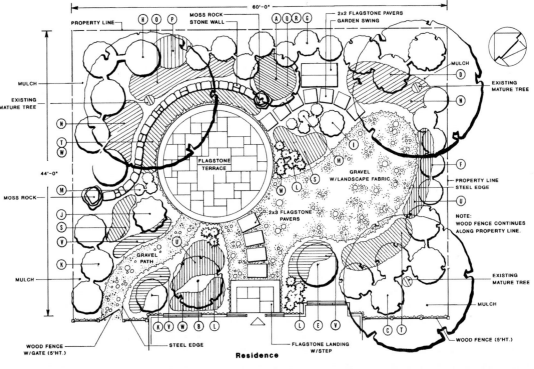

**PLAN VIEW**

# Shady Backyard

Woe to the gardener who has to deal with established tall trees that cast a great deal of shade—a beautiful, colorful backyard is out of the question, right? Wrong! Nothing could be further from the truth, as demonstrated by this artfully designed shade garden. The key to working with large existing trees is in using the shade as an asset, not as a liability, and in choosing shade-loving plants to grow beneath them. If the trees have a very dense canopy, branches can be selectively removed to thin the trees and create filtered shade below.

In this plan, the designer shapes the lawn and beds to respond to the locations of the trees. Note that all but one of the trees are situated in planting beds, not in open lawn. Placing a single tree in the lawn helps to integrate the lawn and planting beds, creating a cohesive design. At the right, the deep planting area is enhanced by pavers, a bench, and a birdbath, creating an inviting, shady retreat. Near the house, a small patio provides a lounging spot; its curving shape echoes the curving form of the planting beds.

Throughout the garden, perennials, woody plants, and groundcovers are arranged in drifts to create a comfortable and serene space. The garden is in constant but ever-changing bloom from early spring through fall, as its special plants—chosen because they thrive in just such a shady setting in their native habitats—go in and out of bloom. Fall brings big splashes of foliage color to complete the year-long show. To provide the finishing carpet to this beautiful and cool shade garden, choose a grass-seed variety selected to tolerate shade.

## Landscape Plan L242 shown in spring
*Designed by Michael J. Opisso*

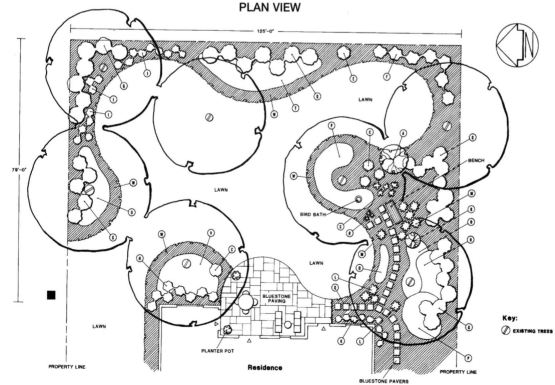

**PLAN VIEW**

125'-0"

79'-0"

LAWN

LAWN

LAWN

LAWN

LAWN

BENCH

BIRD BATH

BLUESTONE PAVING

PLANTER POT

**Residence**

PROPERTY LINE

PROPERTY LINE

BLUESTONE PAVERS

Key:

⊘ EXISTING TREES

N

## REGIONALIZED PLANT LISTS

Because climate and growing conditions vary greatly throughout North America, it is impossible to list here all the plants for this landscape plan that would do well everywhere on the continent. However, you can order a Blueprint Package with plant lists keyed to this plan and selected by expert horticulturists to thrive in your area.

The six-page Blueprint Package features a large-size version of this Plan View, plus a detailed regional Plant and Materials List. It also includes an illustrated list of hundreds of landscape plants suited to your region, in case you wish to make substitutions, as well as planting instructions and plant adaptation maps to ensure professional results with your new landscape.

See page 157 to order your regionalized Blueprint Package.

*Shaded yards need not be dark and dull, as this backyard design demonstrates. Here, beneath the shadows of seven mature trees, a colorful collection of shade-loving shrubs, perennials, and groundcovers flourishes.*

# Shady Wildflower Garden

Native wildflowers, shrubs, and groundcovers decorate this shady site with a parade of colorful flowers. The excitement commences in early spring—before the tree leaves begin to unfold—when the wildflowers bloom in profusion. After this carpet of flowers reaches its peak, the shrubs take over. The designer selects an assortment of native, shade-loving shrubs; many bloom in spring, while others produce unexpected blossoms in early, mid-, and late summer. Though the design's emphasis is on easy-care native plants, which adapt themselves readily to the climate and growing conditions, a few non-native or exotic plants are also included. These combine well with the wildflowers and provide extra structural or textural interest during the off seasons.

Lawn grass usually loses the battle with shade in a tree-filled yard, so the designer installs a curving gravel bed (underlaid with weed-blocking landscape fabric) where a lawn might normally be located. If your trees cast only light shade, you might succeed with a lawn sown with shade-tolerant grass types; selectively thinning tree branches would also help.

The attractive shed provides extra storage space and serves as a potting shed, where you can propagate wildflowers, if you want to indulge a gardening hobby. The attached patio, screened by a small, graceful native tree, offers a private place to relax. The designer blends the shed and attached patio into the landscape by using the same flagstones as in the patio near the house and the stepping stones that meander through the garden.

## Landscape Plan L297 shown in spring

*Designed by David Poplawski*
For Shed Plan JJG107, see page 148

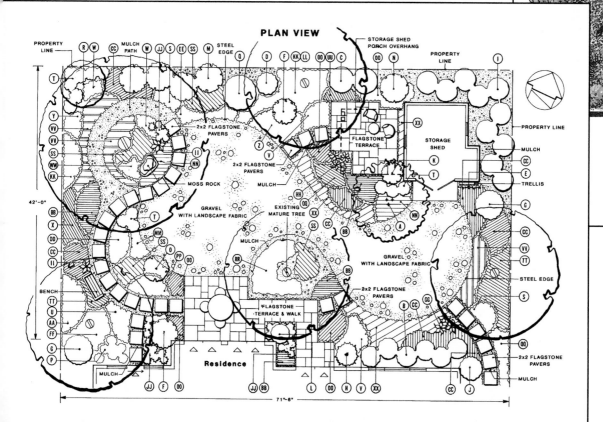

## REGIONALIZED PLANT LISTS

Because climate and growing conditions vary greatly throughout North America, it is impossible to list here all the plants for this landscape plan that would do well everywhere on the continent. However, you can order a Blueprint Package with plant lists keyed to this plan and selected by expert horticulturists to thrive in your area.

The six-page Blueprint Package features a large-size version of this Plan View, plus a detailed regional Plant and Materials List. It also includes an illustrated list of hundreds of landscape plants suited to your region, in case you wish to make substitutions, as well as planting instructions and plant adaptation maps to ensure professional results with your new landscape.

See page 157 to order your regionalized Blueprint Package.

*Here's a flower-filled solution to a tree-filled backyard where lawn grass struggles to survive. An assortment of native shade-loving plants adapts well and blooms from spring through summer.*

# Drought-Resistant Native Plant Garden

This worry-free design makes a perfect planting plan for those needing a second or weekend home, for folks who travel a lot, or for those too busy to fuss over upkeep. During the summer, when most landscapes need regular attention, this one takes care of itself. The landscape is easy-care because drought-tolerant, native plants fill the well-mulched borders, and gravel fills the space normally occupied by a lawn. Homeowners won't have to worry about lawn mowing or watering, even in drought-prone or water-rationed areas.

Of course, it's best to water even these drought-tolerant plants during the first two or three years after initial planting. After that, however, the ones used here won't need more water than the sky delivers. Because they are natives, the trees, shrubs, and flowers used here are adapted to your climate and growing conditions, and are usually problem-free. The only maintenance you'll need to do is occasionally use a leaf blower on the deck and gravel, and cut back the perennials each year.

This distinctive design solves a lot of landscape problems, yet does so with elegance. The expansive low deck is linked to a stately gazebo by a boardwalk, which directs the eye and provides easy walking across the gravel. Located at the end of the boardwalk, yet softened and framed by the asymmetrical placement of the deck tree, the gazebo acts as a dramatic focal point for the overall design. The textures and lines of the wood combine beautifully with the gravel, creating a natural effect that's in keeping with the spirit of the native plants.

## Landscape Plan L299 shown in autumn

*Designed by Jeffrey Diefenbach and Edward D. Georges*
For Gazebo Plan JJG220, see page 149; for Deck Plan JJD125, see page 151

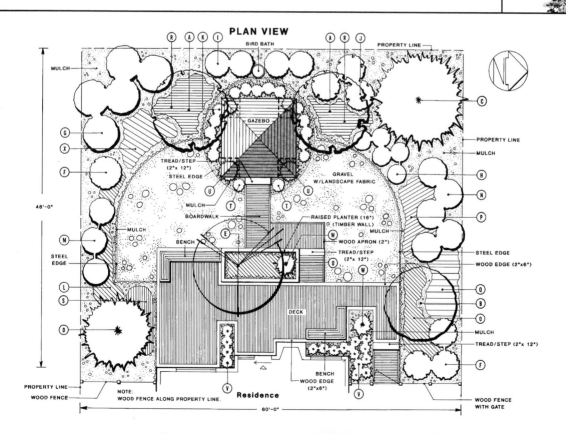

**PLAN VIEW**

MULCH
BIRD BATH
PROPERTY LINE
GAZEBO
C
G
X
F
TREAD/STEP (2"x 12")
STEEL EDGE
PROPERTY LINE
MULCH
GRAVEL W/LANDSCAPE FABRIC
H
N
P
48'-0"
MULCH
BOARDWALK
RAISED PLANTER (16")
(TIMBER WALL)
MULCH
WOOD APRON (2")
MULCH
BENCH
TREAD/STEP (2"x 12")
STEEL EDGE
WOOD EDGE (2"x6")
M
STEEL EDGE
O
B
L
S
D
MULCH
TREAD/STEP (2"x 12")
F
DECK
PROPERTY LINE
WOOD FENCE
NOTE: WOOD FENCE ALONG PROPERTY LINE.
Residence
BENCH WOOD EDGE (2"x6")
WOOD FENCE WITH GATE
60'-0"

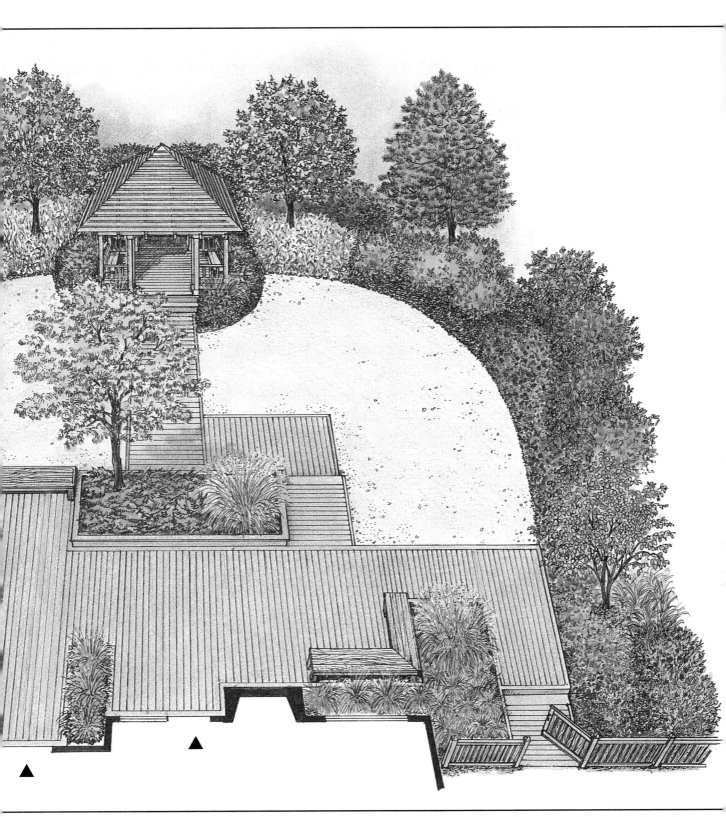

## REGIONALIZED PLANT LISTS

Because climate and growing conditions vary greatly throughout North America, it is impossible to list here all the plants for this landscape plan that would do well everywhere on the continent. However, you can order a Blueprint Package with plant lists keyed to this plan and selected by expert horticulturists to thrive in your area.

The six-page Blueprint Package features a large-size version of this Plan View, plus a detailed regional Plant and Materials List. It also includes an illustrated list of hundreds of landscape plants suited to your region, in case you wish to make substitutions, as well as planting instructions and plant adaptation maps to ensure professional results with your new landscape.

See page 157 to order your regionalized Blueprint Package.

*This native plant garden is both easy-care and ecological. In autumn, ripe berries decorating the tree and shrub branches, and seed heads from the wildflowers and ornamental grasses, provide an excellent food source for migrating birds.*

# Drought-Tolerant Garden

This design proves that "drought tolerant" and "low maintenance" don't have to mean boring. This attractive backyard looks lush, colorful, and inviting, but relies entirely on plants that flourish even if water is scarce. This means you won't spend any time tending to their watering needs once the plantings are established. Even the lawn is planted with a newly developed turf grass that tolerates long periods of drought.

The designer specifies buffalo grass, a native grass of the American West, for the lawn. The grass has fine-textured, grayish green leaf blades, tolerates cold, and needs far less water to remain green and healthy than most lawns. It goes completely dormant during periods of extended drought, but greens up with rain or irrigation. To keep the lawn green throughout summer, all you need do is water occasionally if rainfall doesn't cooperate. And mowing is an occasional activity, too! This slow-growing grass needs mowing only a few times in summer to about one inch high. To keep the grass from spreading into the planting borders—and to reduce weeding and edging chores—the designer calls for a decorative brick mowing strip surrounding the lawn.

Deciduous and evergreen trees and shrubs interplanted with long-blooming flowering perennials—all drought-tolerant—adorn the yard, bringing color every season. Against the fence grow espaliered shrubs, which offer flowers in spring and berries in winter. The vine-covered trellis shades the roomy, angular deck, where you can sit in cool seclusion and relax while your beautiful backyard takes care of itself.

## Landscape Plan L266 shown in summer

*Designed by Damon Scott*
For Deck Plan JJD120, see page 151

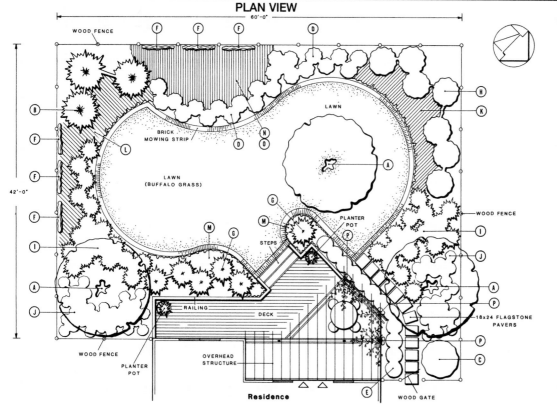

**PLAN VIEW**
60'-0"

WOOD FENCE

LAWN

BRICK
MOWING STRIP

LAWN
(BUFFALO GRASS)

PLANTER
POT

STEPS

42'-0"

WOOD FENCE

RAILING

DECK

WOOD FENCE

PLANTER
POT

OVERHEAD
STRUCTURE

18x24 FLAGSTONE
PAVERS

**Residence**

WOOD GATE

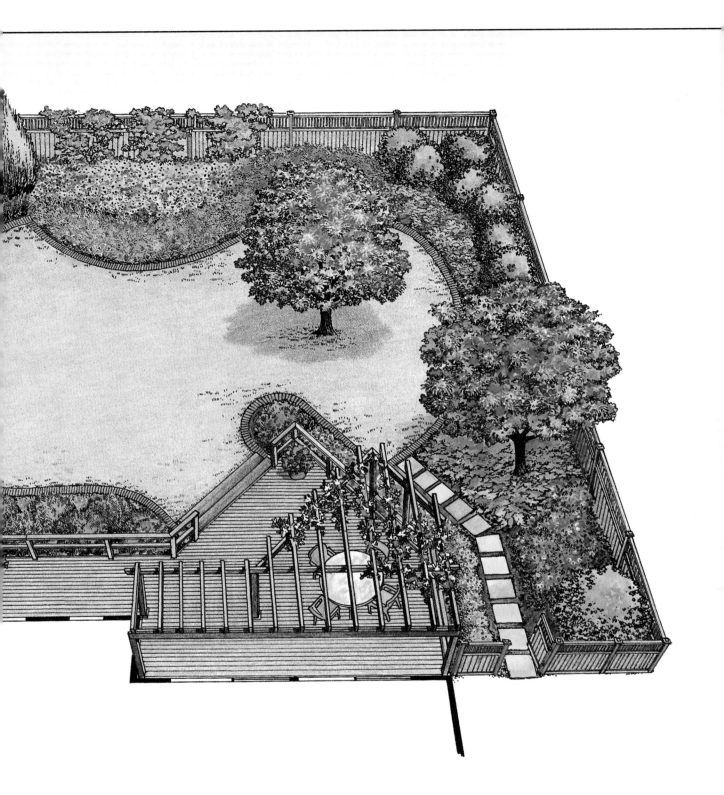

## REGIONALIZED PLANT LISTS

Because climate and growing conditions vary greatly throughout North America, it is impossible to list here all the plants for this landscape plan that would do well everywhere on the continent. However, you can order a Blueprint Package with plant lists keyed to this plan and selected by expert horticulturists to thrive in your area.

The six-page Blueprint Package features a large-size version of this Plan View, plus a detailed regional Plant and Materials List. It also includes an illustrated list of hundreds of landscape plants suited to your region, in case you wish to make substitutions, as well as planting instructions and plant adaptation maps to ensure professional results with your new landscape.

See page 157 to order your regionalized Blueprint Package.

*This environmentally sound landscape plan won't strain the local water supply or burden you with gardening chores, because all the plants used here—from grass to flowers to trees—are easy-care, trouble-free kinds that flourish without frequent rain or irrigation.*

*Low-maintenance water features are the focal points in this walled oasis, just as they were in the original Mediterranean versions. More than just decorative, the cascading water has a calming and cooling effect.*

## REGIONALIZED PLANT LISTS

Because climate and growing conditions vary greatly throughout North America, it is impossible to list here all the plants for this landscape plan that would do well everywhere on the continent. However, you can order a Blueprint Package with plant lists keyed to this plan and selected by expert horticulturists to thrive in your area.

The six-page Blueprint Package features a large-size version of this Plan View, plus a detailed regional Plant and Materials List. It also includes an illustrated list of hundreds of landscape plants suited to your region, in case you wish to make substitutions, as well as planting instructions and plant adaptation maps to ensure professional results with your new landscape.

See page 157 to order your regionalized Blueprint Package.

# Walled Oasis

Originally developed for gardens in the arid regions of the Mediterranean, the walled oasis is a low-maintenance concept that can be adapted to any area and any size property. The relatively small yard shown here is ideally arranged for anyone who enjoys outdoor living more than gardening—yet there are enough plants, both inside the walls and immediately outside the walls, to soften hard surfaces and provide some color and a sense of lushness.

The seven-foot-high walls give homeowners privacy without making them feel confined, thanks to the window openings in the stucco walls and the see-through iron gates. The designer carefully crafts the view through the main window to include a statue, which is positioned at the end of the sight line to create a dramatic focal point. Shrubs with variegated foliage and colorful bark create an unusually beautiful view through the smaller window. Two water features—a fountain and a cascade—provide soothing sound effects and coolness in the heat of summer.

Soft-textured evergreen trees are positioned for privacy, while three horizontally branching flowering trees add drama throughout the year. A hedge bordering the semicircular lawn may be pruned formally (if you're willing to put in the extra effort), or left to grow naturally for a softer appearance. The flagstones in the terrace are set in concrete for easy maintenance. Although the lawn is small enough for quick mowing, it can be replaced with a groundcover that needs no mowing at all.

## Landscape Plan L300 shown in spring
*Designed by Michael Opisso*

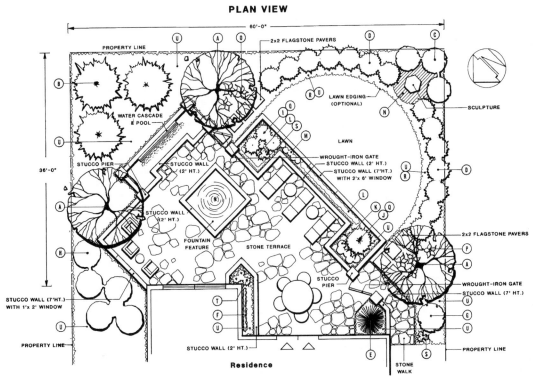

**PLAN VIEW**

60'-0"

PROPERTY LINE

2x2 FLAGSTONE PAVERS

LAWN EDGING
(OPTIONAL)

SCULPTURE

WATER CASCADE
& POOL

LAWN

WROUGHT-IRON GATE
STUCCO WALL (2' HT.)
STUCCO WALL (7'HT.)
WITH 2'x 6' WINDOW

STUCCO PIER

STUCCO WALL
(2' HT.)

36'-0"

STUCCO WALL
(2' HT.)

2x2 FLAGSTONE PAVERS

FOUNTAIN
FEATURE

STONE TERRACE

WROUGHT-IRON GATE
STUCCO WALL (7' HT.)

STUCCO
PIER

STUCCO WALL (7'HT.)
WITH 1'x 2' WINDOW

PROPERTY LINE

PROPERTY LINE

STUCCO WALL (2' HT.)

**Residence**

STONE
WALK

# Lovely Lawnless Backyard

I f you feel like a weekend slave to your lawn and yard, here's a way out: Do away with the green, growing grass; discard the lawn mower; and relax on the weekends, enjoying your backyard as a peaceful haven rather than a nagging maintenance chore.

It's true that lawn acts as an important design feature by creating a plain that carries the eye throughout the garden. It establishes connections between the various garden elements and provides an open feeling while attractively covering the ground. However, lawn requires time and money to maintain. Other materials or plants that require less care can provide a similar effect. Japanese gardens often feature carefully raked gravel to mimic ocean waves; in the Southwest, pretty, colored crushed granite covers many yards; in other areas, low, evergreen groundcovers substitute for lawn grass. In this low-maintenance backyard, the designer incorporates a large deck and patio flanked by a lakelike expanse of dark gravel where a lawn might be. A water-permeable landscape fabric underpins the layer of gravel to stop weeds.

Tall evergreen trees along the rear boundary guarantee privacy, while three large deciduous trees provide plenty of summer shade for the deck and patio. The angular deck features an interesting cutout space for a small viewing garden. The deck steps down to a grade-level brick patio with a circular shape that complements the gravel bed and the planting beds. From the brick terrace, a flagstone pathway leads to a bench positioned in the midst of a bed of flowering perennials. From there, you can reflect upon your garden, your house, and your free time.

## Landscape Plan L268 shown in summer
*Designed by Michael J. Opisso*

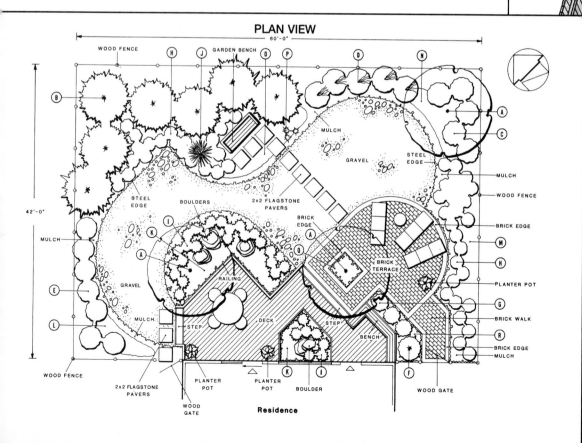

**PLAN VIEW**

60'-0"

42'-0"

WOOD FENCE  GARDEN BENCH

MULCH
GRAVEL
STEEL EDGE
MULCH
WOOD FENCE
BRICK EDGE

STEEL EDGE  BOULDERS  2x2 FLAGSTONE PAVERS  BRICK EDGE

MULCH  GRAVEL  RAILING  BRICK TERRACE  PLANTER POT

BRICK WALK

BRICK EDGE
MULCH

MULCH  STEP  DECK  STEP  BENCH

WOOD FENCE  2x2 FLAGSTONE PAVERS  PLANTER POT  PLANTER POT  BOULDER  WOOD GATE

WOOD GATE

**Residence**

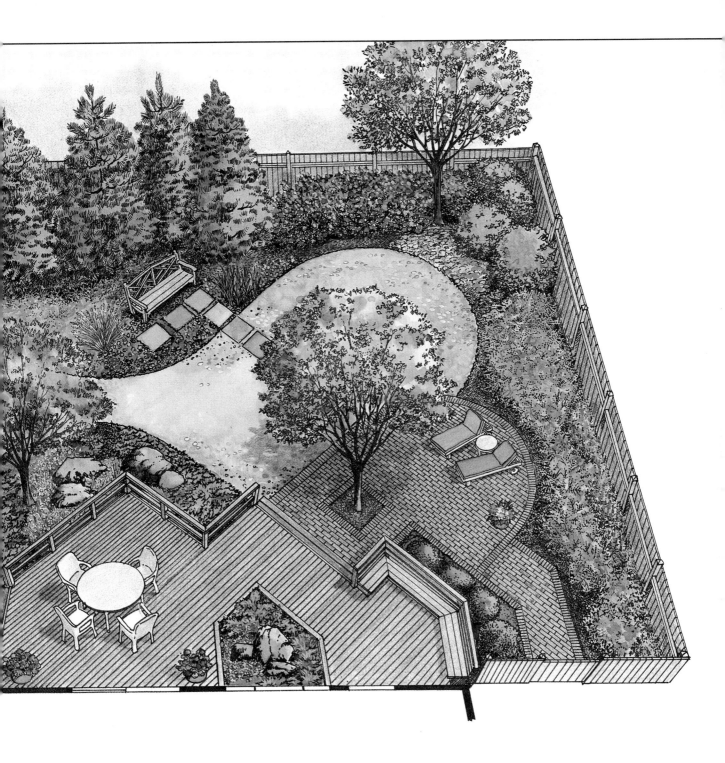

## REGIONALIZED PLANT LISTS

Because climate and growing conditions vary greatly throughout North America, it is impossible to list here all the plants for this landscape plan that would do well everywhere on the continent. However, you can order a Blueprint Package with plant lists keyed to this plan and selected by expert horticulturists to thrive in your area.

The six-page Blueprint Package features a large-size version of this Plan View, plus a detailed regional Plant and Materials List. It also includes an illustrated list of hundreds of landscape plants suited to your region, in case you wish to make substitutions, as well as planting instructions and plant adaptation maps to ensure professional results with your new landscape.

See page 157 to order your regionalized Blueprint Package.

*Eliminate the lawn, and the most time-consuming part of a gardener's maintenance routine is eliminated as well. Easy-care hard surfaces—a gravel bed, a wooden deck, and a brick patio—take the place of lawn, providing inviting spaces for relaxing and enjoying the surrounding flowers and greenery.*

*The spacious deck offers a comfortable vantage point for enjoying the flowers and foliage. Mulched planting beds keep this garden free of most weeds, and if the optional lawn edging is installed, the only regular maintenance chore will be lawn mowing.*

## REGIONALIZED PLANT LISTS

Because climate and growing conditions vary greatly throughout North America, it is impossible to list here all the plants for this landscape plan that would do well everywhere on the continent. However, you can order a Blueprint Package with plant lists keyed to this plan and selected by expert horticulturists to thrive in your area.

The six-page Blueprint Package features a large-size version of this Plan View, plus a detailed regional Plant and Materials List. It also includes an illustrated list of hundreds of landscape plants suited to your region, in case you wish to make substitutions, as well as planting instructions and plant adaptation maps to ensure professional results with your new landscape.

See page 157 to order your regionalized Blueprint Package.

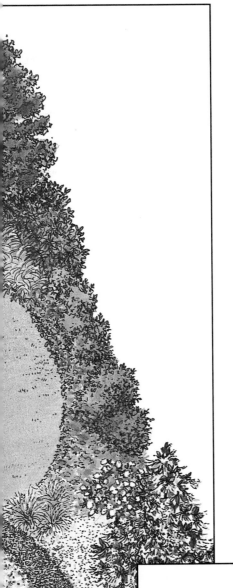

# Naturalistic Flowers and Grasses

A low deck makes an excellent vantage point for surveying this naturalistic garden, which showcases a beautiful selection of flowers and ornamental grasses. To integrate the deck more fully with the landscape and to provide light shade, the designer places several low-maintenance trees in planting pockets in the deck. A graceful arbor positioned straight across from the deck stairs beckons strollers to meander along the semicircular path, where they'll encounter a bench inviting them to sit for a spell. The bench supplies respite and a different perspective from which to admire the garden.

An assortment of plants rings the "figure-eight" lawn, which forms the hub of the landscape. Instead of more traditional groundcovers, drifts of blooming perennials and ornamental grasses blanket the ground. The various plants— chosen for a succession of bloom and carefully interspersed to camouflage the dying foliage of dormant spring bulbs—provide a kaleidoscope of color from season to season.

Besides lawn mowing, the only maintenance you'll need to perform is to cut back and remove the dead foliage once a year in late winter. To reduce upkeep further, a low-care groundcover could be substituted for the turf, and a slightly curving, mulched path installed from the deck stairs to the arbor to accommodate foot traffic.

## Landscape Plan L301 shown in late summer
*Designed by Damon Scott*
For Deck Plan JJD126, see page 151

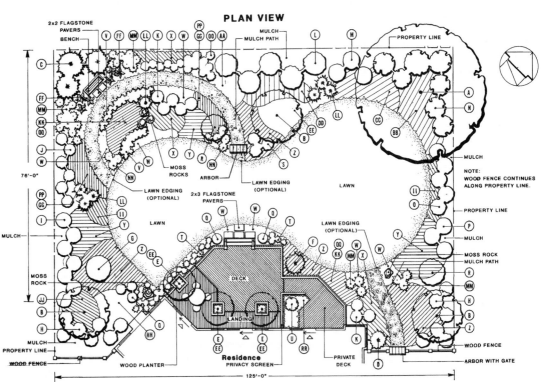

**PLAN VIEW**

This plan re-creates one of nature's great spectacles—a grassy meadow brimming with blooming flowers. A wooden deck rises above the level of the yard so you can appreciate the view from above. Once established, this meadow garden is easy-care and easy on the eye.

## REGIONALIZED PLANT LISTS

Because climate and growing conditions vary greatly throughout North America, it is impossible to list here all the plants for this landscape plan that would do well everywhere on the continent. However, you can order a Blueprint Package with plant lists keyed to this plan and selected by expert horticulturists to thrive in your area.

The six-page Blueprint Package features a large-size version of this Plan View, plus a detailed regional Plant and Materials List. It also includes an illustrated list of hundreds of landscape plants suited to your region, in case you wish to make substitutions, as well as planting instructions and plant adaptation maps to ensure professional results with your new landscape.

See page 157 to order your regionalized Blueprint Package.

# Backyard Meadow Garden

I f you yearn for the look and feel of a flower-drenched meadow, this low-maintenance landscape plan can help you create it in your own backyard. The small formal lawn will need normal mowing maintenance, but once established, the wildflower meadow requires only once-a-year mowing each winter to a height of six inches to keep it blooming and prevent woody plants from invading.

The designer creates the wildflower meadow from native field grass and sun-loving perennial wildflowers—those at home on America's prairies and open meadows. You'll be assured of success with this garden because you start it from container-grown flowers, planted together with seed-sown meadow grass. Unlike flowers in totally seeded meadow gardens, which are difficult at best to get established, this method assures that the flowers become readily established and spread year after year into a gorgeous spectacle of blossoms set off against wavy green grasses. You'll have to weed between plants the first season or two until the desirable flowers and grass become established enough to crowd out weeds.

A rustic, stacked-rail fence, in keeping with the bucolic theme of the garden, separates the manicured lawn from the meadow, serving to tame its wildness just a bit. Plantings near the house include informal plants such as ornamental grasses that echo the wilder look of the plants in the meadow. Drought-tolerant evergreen trees, grouped strategically in the meadow, provide privacy and wind screening while giving the yard a permanent structure and year-round beauty.

## Landscape Plan L258 shown in summer
*Designed by Damon Scott*

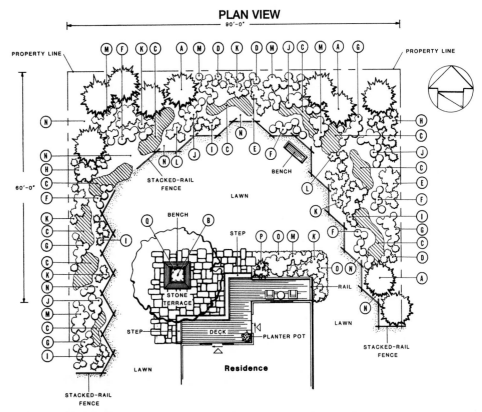

# Easy-Care Natural-Looking Swimming Pool

T he centerpiece of this landscape, which includes several existing mature trees in the background, is a naturalistic swimming pool. Dark paint helps give the pool the look of a real pond, similar to one you might discover in a wilderness clearing.

To the left of the wooden bridge, a gentle waterfall spills into the two-foot-deep children's pool. To the right is a five-foot-deep adults' pool; recessed steps in the wall and rocks strategically placed as handgrips substitute for a ladder, which would mar the illusion of naturalness. Smooth-edged boulders stud the flagstone coping.

The two irregularly shaped lawn areas flank the children's pool—kids can go from splashing in the pool to frolicking on the grass and back again without missing a beat. The shed serves as a storage area for lawn mower, pool equipment, and other tools, or may be turned into a playhouse.

The existing trees give the landscape a head start on privacy. To expand that feeling and to create the effect of a glade, the designer strategically places additional trees around the yard, but well away from the pool. He also clusters well-behaved shrubs, perennials, and groundcovers—some chosen for their colored foliage and others for their seasonal flowers—around the pool, lawn areas, and deck. For easy maintenance, a thick layer of mulch blankets the soil and smothers weeds in the less visible, less accessible perimeter of the yard where groundcover will eventually fill in.

## Landscape Plan L302 shown in summer
*Designed by Edward D. Georges*
For Storage Shed Plan JJG222, see page 149

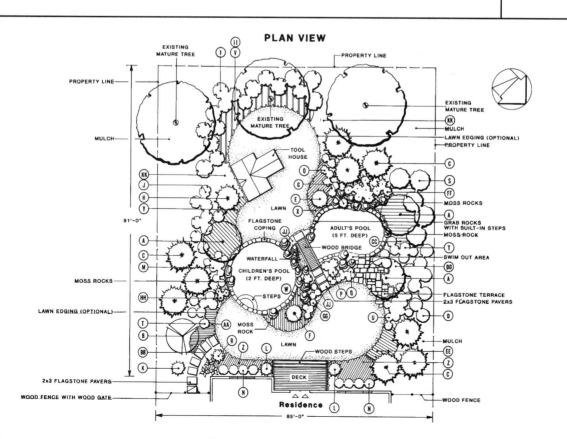

**PLAN VIEW**

EXISTING MATURE TREE

PROPERTY LINE

PROPERTY LINE

EXISTING MATURE TREE

EXISTING MATURE TREE

MULCH

KK
MULCH
LAWN EDGING (OPTIONAL)
PROPERTY LINE

MULCH

TOOL HOUSE

O
G
E
X

C
S
FF
MOSS ROCKS
A
GRAB ROCKS WITH BUILT-IN STEPS
MOSS-ROCK

KK
J
H
Y

LAWN

FLAGSTONE COPING

JJ

ADULT'S POOL (5 FT. DEEP)

CC

WOOD BRIDGE

T
SWIM OUT AREA
DD
A

91'-0"

A
C
M

WATERFALL

CHILDREN'S POOL (2 FT. DEEP)

FLAGSTONE TERRACE 2x3 FLAGSTONE PAVERS

MOSS ROCKS

STEPS

W

P Q

B

LAWN EDGING (OPTIONAL)

HH

JJ
GG

U

T
B

AA
MOSS ROCK

R Z L

F

LAWN

MULCH
EE
Z
C

BB

WOOD STEPS

K

2x3 FLAGSTONE PAVERS

DECK

WOOD FENCE WITH WOOD GATE

N

**Residence**

L

N

WOOD FENCE

85'-0"

## REGIONALIZED PLANT LISTS

Because climate and growing conditions vary greatly throughout North America, it is impossible to list here all the plants for this landscape plan that would do well everywhere on the continent. However, you can order a Blueprint Package with plant lists keyed to this plan and selected by expert horticulturists to thrive in your area.

The six-page Blueprint Package features a large-size version of this Plan View, plus a detailed regional Plant and Materials List. It also includes an illustrated list of hundreds of landscape plants suited to your region, in case you wish to make substitutions, as well as planting instructions and plant adaptation maps to ensure professional results with your new landscape.

See page 157 to order your regionalized Blueprint Package.

*Many of the deciduous and evergreen shrubs in this landscape feature colorful foliage or bark, providing easy-care color and texture through the seasons. Chosen for their small leaves and restrained growth habits, the trees and shrubs won't add to pool maintenance or overrun the lawn areas.*

# Naturalistic Swimming Pool

If you look at this landscape design and ask yourself, "Is that really a swimming pool?" then the designer is to be congratulated because he has succeeded in his intention. Yes, it *is* a swimming pool, but the pool looks more like a natural pond and waterfall—one that you might discover in a clearing in the woods during a hike in the wilderness.

The designer achieves this aesthetically pleasing, natural look by employing several techniques. He creates the pool in an irregular free-form shape and paints it "black," actually a very dark marine blue, to suggest the depths of a lake. Large boulders form the waterfalls, one of which falls from a holding pond set among the boulders. River rock paving—the type of water-worn rocks that line the cool water of a natural spring or a rushing stream—surrounds the front of the pool. The far side of the pool is planted right to the edge, blending the pool into the landscape. If you want to make a splash, you can even dive into this pool—from a diving rock rather than a diving board.

Although the pool is the main attraction here, the rest of the landscape offers a serene setting with abundant floral and foliage interest throughout the year. For security reasons, a wooden stockade fence surrounds the entire backyard, yet the plantings camouflage it well. The irregular kidney shape of the lawn is pleasing to look at and beautifully integrates the naturalistic pool and landscaping into its man-made setting.

## Landscape Plan L248 shown in summer
*Designed by Damon Scott*

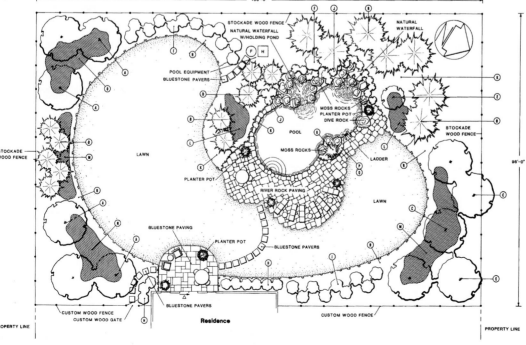

**PLAN VIEW**

STOCKADE WOOD FENCE
NATURAL WATERFALL W/HOLDING POND
NATURAL WATERFALL
POOL EQUIPMENT
BLUESTONE PAVERS
MOSS ROCKS
PLANTER POT
DIVE ROCK
STOCKADE WOOD FENCE
POOL
MOSS ROCKS
LADDER
STOCKADE WOOD FENCE
LAWN
PLANTER POT
RIVER ROCK PAVING
LAWN
BLUESTONE PAVING
PLANTER POT
BLUESTONE PAVERS
BLUESTONE PAVERS
CUSTOM WOOD FENCE
CUSTOM WOOD GATE
CUSTOM WOOD FENCE
**Residence**
PROPERTY LINE
PROPERTY LINE

## REGIONALIZED PLANT LISTS

Because climate and growing conditions vary greatly throughout North America, it is impossible to list here all the plants for this landscape plan that would do well everywhere on the continent. However, you can order a Blueprint Package with plant lists keyed to this plan and selected by expert horticulturists to thrive in your area.

The six-page Blueprint Package features a large-size version of this Plan View, plus a detailed regional Plant and Materials List. It also includes an illustrated list of hundreds of landscape plants suited to your region, in case you wish to make substitutions, as well as planting instructions and plant adaptation maps to ensure professional results with your new landscape.

See page 157 to order your regionalized Blueprint Package.

*Resembling a tranquil country pond high in the mountains, this swimming pool, with its waterfalls, river-rock paving, and border planting, brings a wonderful, natural setting to your own backyard.*

# Japanese-Style Garden

When a busy couple wants a landscape that is distinctive and requires little maintenance, the Japanese-style garden and backyard pictured here are a perfect solution. The essence of a Japanese garden lies in emulating nature through simple, clean lines that do not look contrived. The low, tight hedges underscore the plantings behind them, while providing a contrast in form. Looking straight out from the deck, the perimeter planting is a harmony of shades of green, with interest provided from contrasting textures. Plants throughout require little fuss.

Paving stones border the deck, because, in the Japanese garden, every element has both an aesthetic and a functional purpose. The stones alleviate the wear that would result from stepping directly onto the lawn from the deck, and provide a visual transition between the man-made deck and the natural grass. The pavers act as more than a path; they also provide a sight line to the stone lantern on the left side of the garden.

The deck, like the rest of the landscape, has clean, simple lines, and provides the transition from the home's interior to the garden. It surrounds a viewing garden, one step down. In the Japanese tradition, this miniature landscape mimics a natural scene. The one large moss rock plays an important role—it is situated at the intersection of the stepping-stone paths that lead through the garden. Here a decision must be made as to which way to turn. The stone water basin, a symbolic part of the Japanese tea ceremony, is located near the door to the house, signaling the entrance to a very special place.

## Landscape Plan L241 shown in spring
*Designed by Michael J. Opisso*

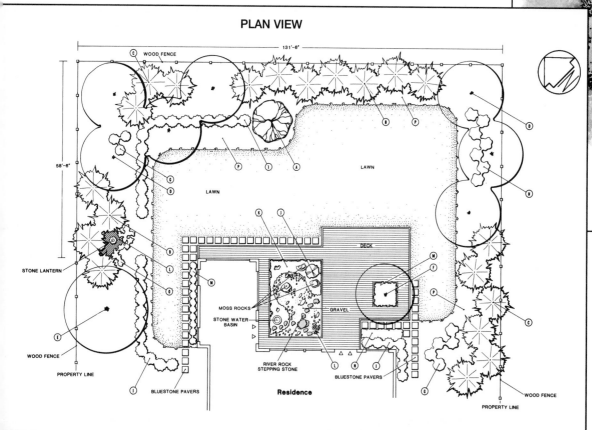

**PLAN VIEW**

## REGIONALIZED PLANT LISTS

Because climate and growing conditions vary greatly throughout North America, it is impossible to list here all the plants for this landscape plan that would do well everywhere on the continent. However, you can order a Blueprint Package with plant lists keyed to this plan and selected by expert horticulturists to thrive in your area.

The six-page Blueprint Package features a large-size version of this Plan View, plus a detailed regional Plant and Materials List. It also includes an illustrated list of hundreds of landscape plants suited to your region, in case you wish to make substitutions, as well as planting instructions and plant adaptation maps to ensure professional results with your new landscape.

See page 157 to order your regionalized Blueprint Package.

*This beautiful Japanese-style garden provides space for outdoor living and entertaining in a tranquil setting. Featuring straight, simple lines, a small lawn, a large deck, and extensive plantings of ground-covers and evergreens, the garden practically cares for itself.*

# Carefree Entertaining

This expansive backyard is designed for entertaining family and friends in a private, relaxing setting. Although the yard measures roughly a quarter of an acre, the overall effect is snug and welcoming. The spacious deck, which runs nearly the width of the house, and the adjoining semicircular brick terrace, allow plenty of room for lounging, dining, and visiting with friends. And there's plenty of room for holding large, outdoor parties—guests can mingle on the deck and patio and even spill over onto the lawn. Providing maximum convenience, the barbecue unit, a service cabinet, and several benches are built in so they're always accessible.

Shaped for efficient mowing, the gracefully curving lawn is large enough to accommodate a badminton court, croquet game, or all the neighborhood children. And fans will find the roofed garden swing, nestled among the plantings, a comfortable grandstand for cheering on their favorite team.

A dramatic purple-leaf weeping tree creates a focal point for the view from the deck and patio. The surrounding plantings include a colorful mix of trees, shrubs, perennials, and bulbs—all chosen for their tidiness or subdued growth. Mulch, which blankets the garden floor to keep down weeds and promote healthy plant growth, is another work-saving measure.

## Landscape Plan L303 shown in summer
*Designed by Maria Morrison*
For Deck Plan JJD118, see page 150
For Garden Swing Plan JJG237, see page 149

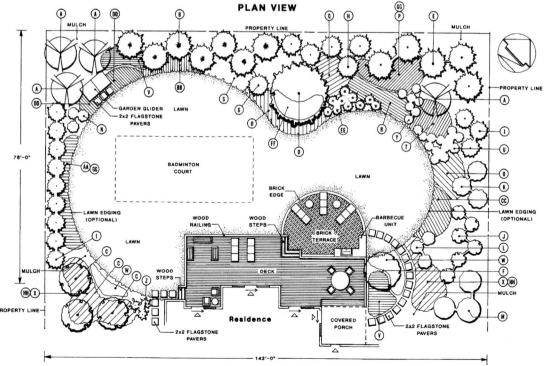

PLAN VIEW

## REGIONALIZED PLANT LISTS

Because climate and growing conditions vary greatly throughout North America, it is impossible to list here all the plants for this landscape plan that would do well everywhere on the continent. However, you can order a Blueprint Package with plant lists keyed to this plan and selected by expert horticulturists to thrive in your area.

The six-page Blueprint Package features a large-size version of this Plan View, plus a detailed regional Plant and Materials List. It also includes an illustrated list of hundreds of landscape plants suited to your region, in case you wish to make substitutions, as well as planting instructions and plant adaptation maps to ensure professional results with your new landscape.

See page 157 to order your regionalized Blueprint Package.

*Even when there's no action on the playing court, there's something exciting going on in this garden. Designed for year-round interest, the mixed plantings bordering the lawn were chosen for colorful flowers, foliage, or fruit, as well as easy upkeep.*

*There's a lot to see from this bi-level deck, since the designer planned a garden that's beautiful throughout the year. Evergreens at the property border provide enclosure and privacy and don't pose clean-up problems.*

## REGIONALIZED PLANT LISTS

Because climate and growing conditions vary greatly throughout North America, it is impossible to list here all the plants for this landscape plan that would do well everywhere on the continent. However, you can order a Blueprint Package with plant lists keyed to this plan and selected by expert horticulturists to thrive in your area.

The six-page Blueprint Package features a large-size version of this Plan View, plus a detailed regional Plant and Materials List. It also includes an illustrated list of hundreds of landscape plants suited to your region, in case you wish to make substitutions, as well as planting instructions and plant adaptation maps to ensure professional results with your new landscape.

See page 157 to order your regionalized Blueprint Package.

D esigned to be enjoyed rather than slaved over, this backyard paradise offers a variety of outdoor living spaces. The large deck is designed with two levels to accommodate uneven terrain and provide easy-access from the split-level house. The two levels of the deck act as separate outdoor rooms: From the large, higher level, you can enjoy a wonderful view of the entire property with plenty of room for guests to walk around and mingle. The lower level is more intimate; three vase-shaped trees provide shade and a sense of privacy while framing the view.

A gracefully curving flagstone walk leads from the deck to a stone terrace and gazebo—additional outdoor rooms perfect for relaxing or entertaining. (The walkway doubles as a mowing strip, making the relatively small lawn even easier to mow.) When seated in the sun on the patio, or in the shade of the gazebo, you can enjoy the music created by the windchime sculpture—an eye- and ear-catching focal point beside the gazebo. A living sculpture, in the form of a weeping evergreen, visually balances the chimes. Both are set in gravel beds for added emphasis.

The plantings require little routine care because the many evergreens that fill out the design don't shed a litter of leaves and don't need regular pruning. Flowering shrubs and perennials create a changing show of blossoms from spring through fall, while the evergreens provide a dependable backdrop of greenery and varied textures. You can plant your choice of easy-care annuals in the deck planters.

## Landscape Plan L304 shown in summer
*Designed by Jim Morgan*
For Deck Plan JJD122, see page 151; for Gazebo Plan JJG108, see page 148

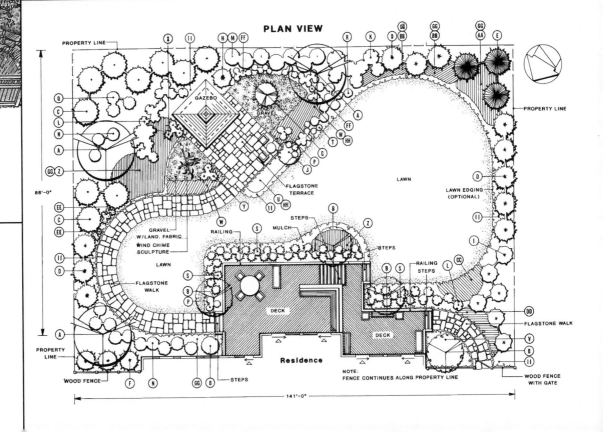

*You'll spend many more hours just relaxing in this backyard retreat than you will taking care of it. Since there's no lawn, you'll escape weekly lawn mowing, and will even be able to leave the garden untended during extended vacations.*

## REGIONALIZED PLANT LISTS

Because climate and growing conditions vary greatly throughout North America, it is impossible to list here all the plants for this landscape plan that would do well everywhere on the continent. However, you can order a Blueprint Package with plant lists keyed to this plan and selected by expert horticulturists to thrive in your area.

The six-page Blueprint Package features a large-size version of this Plan View, plus a detailed regional Plant and Materials List. It also includes an illustrated list of hundreds of landscape plants suited to your region, in case you wish to make substitutions, as well as planting instructions and plant adaptation maps to ensure professional results with your new landscape.

See page 157 to order your regionalized Blueprint Package.

# Effortless Informality

Your cares melt away when you enter this very private and tranquil garden through the vine-covered arbor. The designer sites an informal flagstone terrace with two seating areas in a sea of evergreen groundcover, entirely eliminating a lawn and making the garden about as carefree as it can be. Evergreens on the property border create privacy, while airy trees—selected because they cast light shade and are easy to clean up after—create a lacy overhead canopy. The overall effect is serene.

A half-circle rock wall, built of small, moss-covered boulders, sets off the larger of the two seating areas and gives dimension to the area. (Five moss rocks on the opposite side of the patio echo and balance the wall.) Several types of perennials spill over the top and sprout from the crevices of the wall, decorating the area with their dainty flowers and foliage and creating a soft, natural look. Large drifts of spring bulbs and other perennials make lovely splashes of color where they grow through the groundcover. Flowering shrubs—many of which also display evergreen leaves—give the garden year-round structure and interest, while offering easy-care floral beauty.

The lack of a lawn makes this garden especially easy to care for. The groundcover absorbs most of the leaves that drop from the deciduous trees in autumn, and the terrace can be quickly swept or blown free of leaves and debris, as needed. All you'll need to do is cut off the dead tops of the perennials once a year in late winter.

## Landscape Plan L305 shown in summer
*Designed by Michael Opisso*

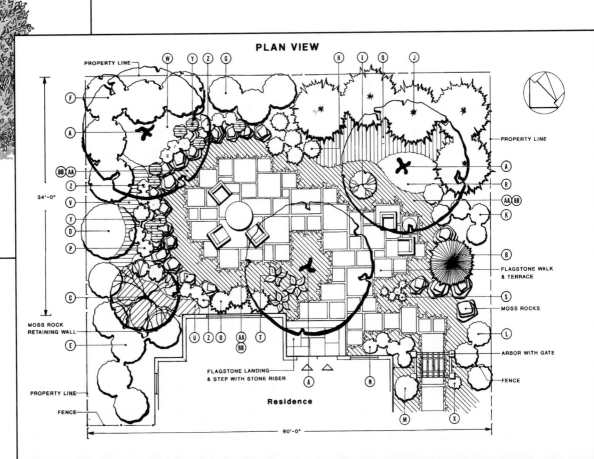

**PLAN VIEW**

PROPERTY LINE
PROPERTY LINE
34'-0"
MOSS ROCK
RETAINING WALL
PROPERTY LINE
FENCE

FLAGSTONE WALK & TERRACE
MOSS ROCKS
ARBOR WITH GATE
FENCE

FLAGSTONE LANDING & STEP WITH STONE RISER

Residence

60'-0"

*Nature lovers will delight in the abundant number of birds that will flock to this beautiful garden. An attractive collection of berried plants and evergreens offers food and shelter for the wildlife, while creating a handsome, pastoral setting.*

## REGIONALIZED PLANT LISTS

Because climate and growing conditions vary greatly throughout North America, it is impossible to list here all the plants for this landscape plan that would do well everywhere on the continent. However, you can order a Blueprint Package with plant lists keyed to this plan and selected by expert horticulturists to thrive in your area.

The six-page Blueprint Package features a large-size version of this Plan View, plus a detailed regional Plant and Materials List. It also includes an illustrated list of hundreds of landscape plants suited to your region, in case you wish to make substitutions, as well as planting instructions and plant adaptation maps to ensure professional results with your new landscape.

See page 157 to order your regionalized Blueprint Package.

# Garden to Attract Birds

There is no better way to wake up in the morning than to the sound of songbirds in the garden. Wherever you live, you will be surprised at the number and variety of birds you can attract by offering them a few basic necessities—water, shelter, nesting spots, and food. Birds need water for drinking and bathing. They need shrubs and trees, especially evergreens, for shelter and nesting. Edge spaces—open areas with trees nearby for quick protection—provide ground feeders with foraging places, while plants with berries and nuts offer other natural sources of food.

The design presented here contains all the necessary elements to attract birds to the garden. The shrubs and trees are chosen especially to provide a mix of evergreen and deciduous species. All of these, together with the masses of flowering perennials, bear seeds, nuts, or berries, are known to appeal to birds. The berry show looks quite pretty, too, until the birds gobble them up! Planted densely enough for necessary shelter, the bird-attracting plants create a lovely private backyard that's enjoyable throughout the seasons.

The birdbath is located in the lawn so it will be in the sun. A naturalistic pond provides water in a more protected setting. The birdhouses and feeders aren't really necessary—though they may be the icing on the cake when it comes to luring the largest number of birds—because the landscape provides abundant natural food and shelter. Outside one of the main windows of the house, a birdfeeder hangs from a small flowering tree, providing an up-close view of your feathered friends.

## Landscape Plan L245 shown in autumn
*Designed by Michael J. Opisso*

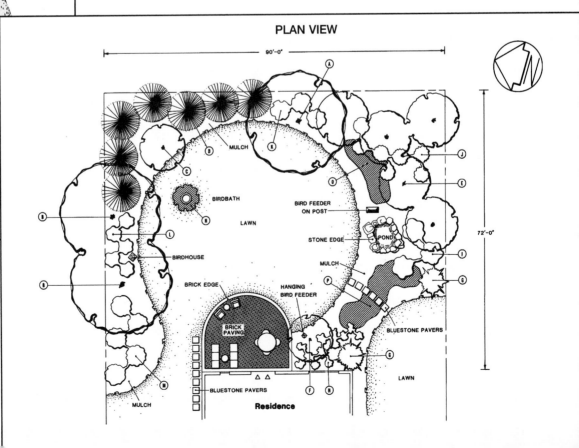

**PLAN VIEW**

90'-0"

72'-0"

MULCH

BIRDBATH

LAWN

BIRD FEEDER ON POST

STONE EDGE

POND

MULCH

BIRDHOUSE

BRICK EDGE

HANGING BIRD FEEDER

BLUESTONE PAVERS

BRICK PAVING

BLUESTONE PAVERS

LAWN

MULCH

Residence

# Songbird Garden

This naturalistic garden plan relies upon several different features to attract as many different species of birds as possible. A songbird's basic needs include food, water, and shelter, but this backyard plan offers luxury accommodations not found in every yard, and also provides the maximum opportunity for birds and bird-watchers to observe each other. Special features provide for specific birds; for example, the rotting log attracts woodpeckers and the dusting area will be used gratefully by birds to free themselves of parasites. In addition to plants that produce plentiful berries and seeds, the designer includes a ground feeder to lure mourning doves, cardinals, and other birds that prefer to eat off the ground. The birdhouse located in the shade of the specimen tree to the rear of the garden suits a wide variety of songbirds.

The angular deck nestles attractively into the restful circular shapes of the garden. The designer encloses the deck amidst the bird-attracting plantings to maximize close-up observation opportunities and create an intimate setting. Two other sitting areas welcome bird-watchers into the garden. A bench positioned on a small patio under the shade of a graceful flowering tree provides a relaxing spot to sit and contemplate the small garden pool and the melody of a low waterfall. Another bench—this one situated in the sun—may be reached by strolling along a path of wood-rounds on the opposite side of the yard. Both wildlife and people will find this backyard a very special retreat.

## Landscape Plan L275 shown in spring

*Designed by David Poplawski*
For Deck Plan JJD115, see page 150; for Birdhouse Plans, see page 147

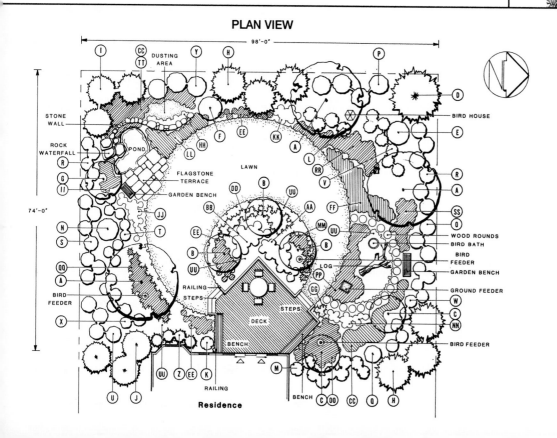

**PLAN VIEW**

98'-0"

74'-0"

STONE WALL

ROCK WATERFALL

POND

DUSTING AREA

FLAGSTONE TERRACE

GARDEN BENCH

LAWN

BIRD HOUSE

WOOD ROUNDS
BIRD BATH
BIRD FEEDER
GARDEN BENCH
GROUND FEEDER

BIRD FEEDER

LOG

RAILING
STEPS

STEPS

DECK

BENCH

RAILING

BENCH

BIRD FEEDER

**Residence**

## REGIONALIZED PLANT LISTS

Because climate and growing conditions vary greatly throughout North America, it is impossible to list here all the plants for this landscape plan that would do well everywhere on the continent. However, you can order a Blueprint Package with plant lists keyed to this plan and selected by expert horticulturists to thrive in your area.

The six-page Blueprint Package features a large-size version of this Plan View, plus a detailed regional Plant and Materials List. It also includes an illustrated list of hundreds of landscape plants suited to your region, in case you wish to make substitutions, as well as planting instructions and plant adaptation maps to ensure professional results with your new landscape.

See page 157 to order your regionalized Blueprint Package.

*This large, naturalistic backyard design creates a wonderful environment for attracting a wide range of bird species, because it offers a plentiful supply of natural food, water, and shelter. The deck and garden benches invite people to observe and listen to the songbirds in comfort.*

*In this romantic garden devoted to especially sweet-smelling shrubs, you'll find special corners—an arbor, a patio, and a wooden bench—isolated for your pleasure. The repeated curves of the lawn, patio, and paths reflect each other to create a harmonious and restful space, where family and friends can enjoy the delightful sights and scents permeating the air.*

## REGIONALIZED PLANT LISTS

Because climate and growing conditions vary greatly throughout North America, it is impossible to list here all the plants for this landscape plan that would do well everywhere on the continent. However, you can order a Blueprint Package with plant lists keyed to this plan and selected by expert horticulturists to thrive in your area.

The six-page Blueprint Package features a large-size version of this Plan View, plus a detailed regional Plant and Materials List. It also includes an illustrated list of hundreds of landscape plants suited to your region, in case you wish to make substitutions, as well as planting instructions and plant adaptation maps to ensure professional results with your new landscape.

See page 157 to order your regionalized Blueprint Package.

# *Fragrant Shrub Garden*

If you're the kind of gardener whose nose is always buried in the nearest blossom and feels disappointed to find a gorgeous rose as scentless as it is beautiful, this landscape plan might be just the one for you. The designer makes every effort to choose the most fragrant plants available to fill this low-maintenance garden with sweet and spicy aromas from spring through fall.

Curving paths and romantic, secluded sitting areas invite you to stroll and rest among the scented plants. Sit under the arbor and enjoy the intensely fragrant flowering shrubs directly behind you in spring and the heady scent of climbing roses overhead in summer. In fall, the delicate perfume of the late bloomers will delight you. Even if you don't move from the patio, the sweet, pervasive perfume from the inconspicuous flowers of the surrounding shrubs will delight you on warm July evenings for years to come.

You'll find the garden is as easy to care for as it is fragrant because the designer selects low-maintenance shrubs (including many dwarf types), trees, and groundcovers, instead of labor-intensive annuals and perennials, to provide color and fragrance. The carefully arranged shrubs have plenty of room to grow without crowding each other or outgrowing their spaces, so you won't have to worry about extensive pruning chores. Much of the area that would be lawn in most yards is devoted here to the brick patio and shrub borders, allowing more kinds of plants to be included and minimizing lawn-care chores. Maintaining this landscape proves to be surprisingly easy—it won't require you to make it your life's work even though it might look that way.

## Landscape Plan L267 shown in summer
*Designed by Tom Nordloh*
For Arbor Plan, see page 147

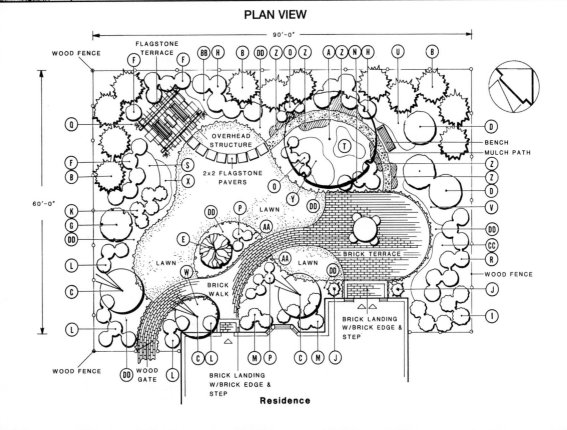

**PLAN VIEW**

# Shady Flower Border

Y̶ou'll never again bemoan the fact that nothing will grow under the shade of the large trees in your backyard if you plant this beautiful shady flower border. Lawn grass needs full sun and struggles to grow under trees. So why not plant something that flourishes in the shade and looks a whole lot prettier! This charming flower border, featuring shade-loving perennials and ferns, fits under the existing trees along the property line of a shady backyard. Blooming from spring through fall, the border delights with its everchanging display of flowers.

The garden's floor features a low-spreading evergreen groundcover through which the flowering perennials grow. The groundcover keeps the garden pretty year-round, even in winter when the perennials are dormant, and won't compete significantly with them for nutrients or water. Large rocks and boulders also give the area year-round structure and interest, as does the bench, which invites you to sit down and enjoy the pretty scene.

The designer shows this garden against a fence along the property border, but you could plant the garden in front of a hedge or other shrubbery and place it along any side of your yard. If your property isn't as large as the one shown here, the garden could easily be shortened by eliminating the corner containing the bench and ending the border with the grouping of three rocks to the left of the bench.

**Landscape Plan L277 shown in summer**
*Designed by Michael J. Opisso*

**PLAN VIEW**

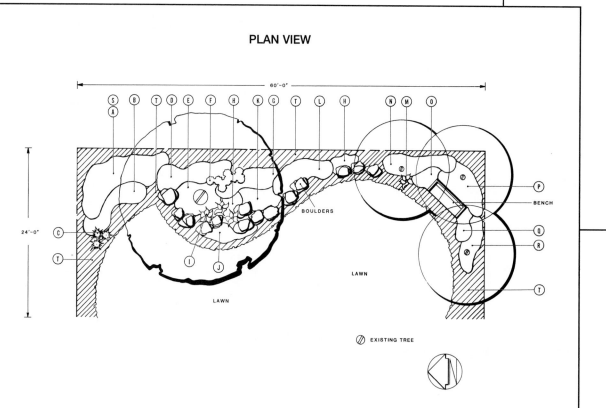

## REGIONALIZED PLANT LISTS

Because climate and growing conditions vary greatly throughout North America, it is impossible to list here all the plants for this landscape plan that would do well everywhere on the continent. However, you can order a Blueprint Package with plant lists keyed to this plan and selected by expert horticulturists to thrive in your area.

The six-page Blueprint Package features a large-size version of this Plan View, plus a detailed regional Plant and Materials List. It also includes an illustrated list of hundreds of landscape plants suited to your region, in case you wish to make substitutions, as well as planting instructions and plant adaptation maps to ensure professional results with your new landscape.

See page 157 to order your regionalized Blueprint Package.

*This garden of shade-loving plants flourishes under trees, where grass struggles to survive. Be sure to keep the plants healthy by providing plenty of water and fertilizer, especially if the garden plants compete for moisture and nutrients with thirsty tree roots. Thin out selected tree branches if the shade they cast is very dense.*

*Brimming with easy-care flowers from spring through fall, this low-maintenance flower border evokes the spirit of an English garden, but doesn't require a staff to take care of it.*

## REGIONALIZED PLANT LISTS

Because climate and growing conditions vary greatly throughout North America, it is impossible to list here all the plants for this landscape plan that would do well everywhere on the continent. However, you can order a Blueprint Package with plant lists keyed to this plan and selected by expert horticulturists to thrive in your area.

The six-page Blueprint Package features a large-size version of this Plan View, plus a detailed regional Plant and Materials List. It also includes an illustrated list of hundreds of landscape plants suited to your region, in case you wish to make substitutions, as well as planting instructions and plant adaptation maps to ensure professional results with your new landscape.

See page 157 to order your regionalized Blueprint Package.

# Easy-Care English Border

A flower-filled garden created in the romantic style of an English border need not require a tremendous amount of care, as this lovely design illustrates. The designer carefully selects unfussy bulbs and perennials, and a few flowering shrubs. All are disease- and insect-resistant, noninvasive, and don't need staking or other regular maintenance to look their best. A balanced number of spring-, summer-, and fall-blooming perennials ensures that the border looks exciting through the entire growing season. Because English gardens are famous for their gorgeous, old-fashioned roses, the designer includes several rosebushes, but chooses a type that doesn't succumb to bugs and mildew.

Hedges form a backdrop for most English flower gardens; the designer plants an informal evergreen hedge here to save on pruning chores. A generous mulched path runs between the background flowers and the hedge, so it's easy to tend the hedge and the flowers at the back of the border. Edging, installed around the periphery of the border, keeps lawn grass from invading the garden and creating a nuisance.

You can plant this flower border along any sunny side of your property. Imagine it along the back of your yard, where you can view it from your kitchen window or from a patio or deck. It would even look wonderful along one side of the front yard, or planted with the hedge bordering the front of your property and providing privacy from the street.

## Landscape Plan L306 shown in summer
*Designed by Maria Morrison*

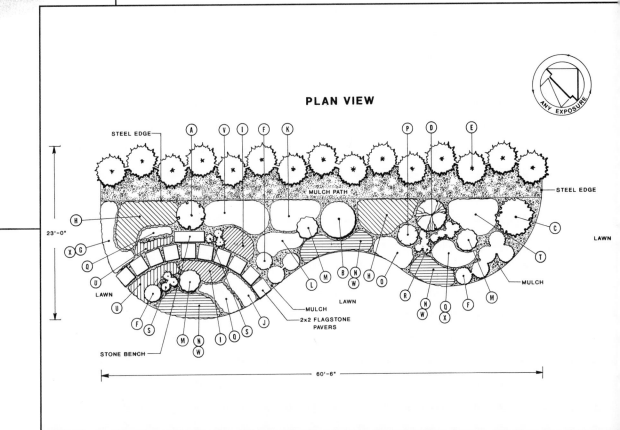

PLAN VIEW

ANY EXPOSURE

STEEL EDGE

MULCH PATH

STEEL EDGE

LAWN

23'-0"

LAWN

LAWN

MULCH

MULCH

2x2 FLAGSTONE PAVERS

STONE BENCH

60'-6"

# Easy-Care Mixed Border

W hen small trees, flowering shrubs, perennials, and groundcovers are planted together in a garden, the result is a lovely mixed border that looks great throughout the year. The trees and shrubs—both evergreen and deciduous types—give the garden structure and form in winter, while also offering decorative foliage and flowers during other seasons. Perennials and bulbs occupy large spaces between groupings of the woody plants, and contribute leaf texture and floral color to the ever-changing scene.

Even though this border contains a lot of plants, it is easy to care for. That's part of the beauty of a mixed border—the woody plants in it are long-lived and need little pruning, if allowed to grow naturally. By limiting the number of perennials and blanketing the ground with weed-smothering groundcovers, you can keep maintenance to a minimum without sacrificing beauty.

You can install this mixed border in a sunny location almost anywhere on your property, though it's intended to run along the back of an average-sized lot. The curved outlines add depth and drama to the design, making it fascinating from any angle. If your property is larger or smaller than the one in this plan, you can alter the design by either increasing or decreasing the number of plants in each grouping.

## Landscape Plan L307 shown in spring
*Designed by Jim Morgan*

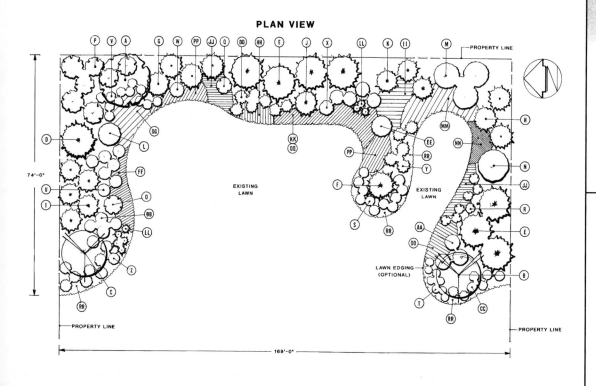

PLAN VIEW

PROPERTY LINE

EXISTING LAWN

EXISTING LAWN

LAWN EDGING (OPTIONAL)

74'-0"

169'-0"

PROPERTY LINE

PROPERTY LINE

## REGIONALIZED PLANT LISTS

Because climate and growing conditions vary greatly throughout North America, it is impossible to list here all the plants for this landscape plan that would do well everywhere on the continent. However, you can order a Blueprint Package with plant lists keyed to this plan and selected by expert horticulturists to thrive in your area.

The six-page Blueprint Package features a large-size version of this Plan View, plus a detailed regional Plant and Materials List. It also includes an illustrated list of hundreds of landscape plants suited to your region, in case you wish to make substitutions, as well as planting instructions and plant adaptation maps to ensure professional results with your new landscape.

See page 157 to order your regionalized Blueprint Package.

*Evergreen and deciduous shrubs and small trees, mixed with drifts of bulbs and flowering perennials, create an ever-changing border that's gorgeous every month of the year.*

# Easy-Care Shrub Border

Nothing beats flowering shrubs and trees for an easy-care show of flowers and foliage throughout the seasons. This lovely garden includes shrubs that bloom at various times of the year—from late winter right into autumn—so that blossoms will always be decorating this garden. In autumn, the leaves of the deciduous shrubs turn flaming shades of yellow, gold, orange, and red. (These colors appear even more brilliant when juxtaposed against the deep greens of the evergreen shrubs.) During the coldest months, when the flowers and fall foliage are finally finished, many of the plants feature glossy red berries or evergreen leaves that take on deep burgundy hues.

The designer balances the border with a tall evergreen and two flowering trees, which serve as anchors at the borders' widest points. Most shrubs are grouped in all-of-a-kind drifts to create the most impact—low, spreading types in the front and taller ones in the back—but several specimens appear alone as eye-catching focal points. A few large drifts of easy-care, long-blooming perennials, interplanted with spring-flowering bulbs, break up the shrubbery to give a variety of textures and forms.

Designed for the back of an average-sized lot, this easy-care border can be located in any sunny area of your property. It makes a perfect addition to any existing property with only a high-maintenance lawn and little other landscaping. The design adds year-round interest, creates privacy, and reduces maintenance.

## Landscape Plan L308 shown in spring
*Designed by Salvatore A. Masullo*

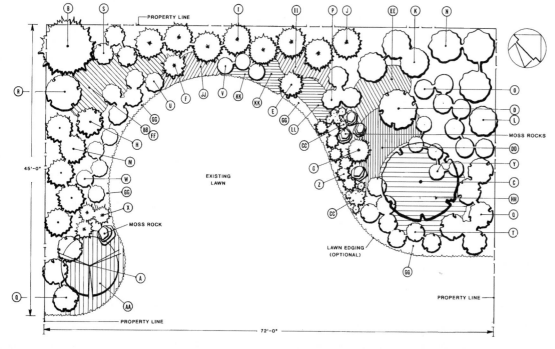

**PLAN VIEW**

EXISTING LAWN

MOSS ROCKS

MOSS ROCK

LAWN EDGING (OPTIONAL)

PROPERTY LINE

45'-0"

72'-0"

## REGIONALIZED PLANT LISTS

Because climate and growing conditions vary greatly throughout North America, it is impossible to list here all the plants for this landscape plan that would do well everywhere on the continent. However, you can order a Blueprint Package with plant lists keyed to this plan and selected by expert horticulturists to thrive in your area.

The six-page Blueprint Package features a large-size version of this Plan View, plus a detailed regional Plant and Materials List. It also includes an illustrated list of hundreds of landscape plants suited to your region, in case you wish to make substitutions, as well as planting instructions and plant adaptation maps to ensure professional results with your new landscape.

See page 157 to order your regionalized Blueprint Package.

*When easy-care, disease- and insect-resistant shrubs are used to create a border, and allowed to grow naturally without excessive pruning, the result is a beautiful, practically maintenance-free garden.*

# CHAPTER 5

# Installing Your Easy-Care Landscape

*Here's How to Adapt Any of These Landscape Designs to Your Site*

Design: Conni Cross

The plans in this book were designed to assist you in landscaping your property—in making the landscape as beautiful, special, and livable as it can be. There are several ways the professionally designed plans included here can help to make your dream landscape a reality. If your yard and your family's needs match one of the designs in this book, you can use that design exactly or almost as it appears on the pages. Where slight variations in the size of your yard or in the layout of your home occur, you can easily adapt the plans—this chapter tells you how. Or you may want to follow the plans as a basic recipe, using your own imagination and creativity to customize a plan to your home.

If you've never designed a landscape, it's understandable that you may not feel comfortable about how to begin. You may be concerned that you lack the necessary creativity, knowledge, or experience. If this is in the back of your mind, don't worry, because you can quite easily adapt the designs presented in this book.

Study the plans and the renderings in Chapters 3 and 4, concentrating on the ones you think may look attractive on your property. Select the one with the landscaping style you like the most, and then proceed with any necessary adjustments as outlined in this chapter.

## Choosing Plants to Carry Out the Plans

The plans in this book indicate the layout and placement of plants and hardscape, but they don't detail the exact names of the plants used to carry out the designs. That's because landscape plants are adapted to different climates, and very few are suited to all areas. For any of the plans featured here, you can order a complete set of blueprints with a plant list selected specifically to do well in your region. (See pages 154-157 to order.) Or you can choose your favorite locally adapted plants to carry out the design. Even though the plans in this book don't indicate the exact plants to use, you can read the template (see illustration on page 138) to tell where the designer chose to place different types and sizes of trees, shrubs, groundcovers, and perennials, so you won't go wrong.

*This entrance planting gets its eye-catching appeal from the mixed planting of trees, shrubs, and vines that gives it year-round color and structure. Easy-care annuals fill in under the central tree and spill out onto the walk to provide long-lasting splashes of color.*

The plan itself solves the design problem of artistically laying out the landscape and balancing sizes and shapes to complement the yard. The designer figured out where to locate outdoor living and recreation areas, and decided where and how to best direct people gracefully through the yard. This basic layout will remain the same regardless of the particular plants you choose to include. Make sure, however, that the plants are in keeping with the spirit of the landscape design, as shown in the color illustration, and aren't likely to outgrow their allotted space.

## Creating Your Landscape Plan

A drawing that accurately depicts the size, shape, and important features of your new landscape is an essential requirement before installing a landscape design. There is no other way to test—before planting—whether a tree, once mature, will be too close to the house, or a shrub will crowd a walk. The process of making the drawing also tends to generate ideas, and certainly it's quicker to experiment with a pencil and an eraser than with a shovel and your muscles. The time you spend putting your plan on paper pays off later.

### Plan-Making Tools

You'll need tracing paper, pencils, an eraser, a scale ruler, and several large sheets of graph paper. You can find graph paper in various sizes, but 18 x 24-inch sheets are the most useful because they're the same size as the blueprints for the plans in this book. Although a triangular-shaped scale ruler isn't essential, you'll find that it makes measuring to scale much quicker. To make your plan as professional looking as possible, you may also want to have handy a T-square, a template of landscape symbols, and a compass.

### Begin With a Survey

You'll need an accurate drawing of your existing property. The best way to start is with your official property survey. If you didn't get a copy when you purchased the property, your city building department should have one on file. If not, you'll need to measure the property boundaries yourself or have the land professionally surveyed.

Draw your plot plan using a convenient scale—usually 1 inch of drawing representing either 4 feet ($\frac{1}{4}$ scale) or 8 feet ($\frac{1}{8}$ scale) of property. (If the scale is too compressed—less than $\frac{1}{8}$ scale—details become smaller and more difficult to visualize.) On the other hand, if the scale is too large, the plan may not fit on the paper. If you plan to order a set of blueprints for one of the plans shown in this book, you'll find it convenient to use the same scale as the plans you get. Plans of large properties employ a $\frac{1}{8}$ scale, and those of smaller properties use a $\frac{1}{4}$ scale.

On tracing paper, accurately redraw your survey, enlarging it to fit the chosen scale, if need be. Then add all existing and permanent features that you want to keep, such as pathways, a patio or deck, and walls. Next, draw in all existing trees, shrubs, and garden areas that you want to keep. (This will be easy for a newly built home on an otherwise empty property.) Once you've included these permanent landscape features on the plot plan, note the locations of all doors and windows. Don't guess at the dimensions. Use a 50- or 100-foot tape measure and work as precisely as you can. Finally,

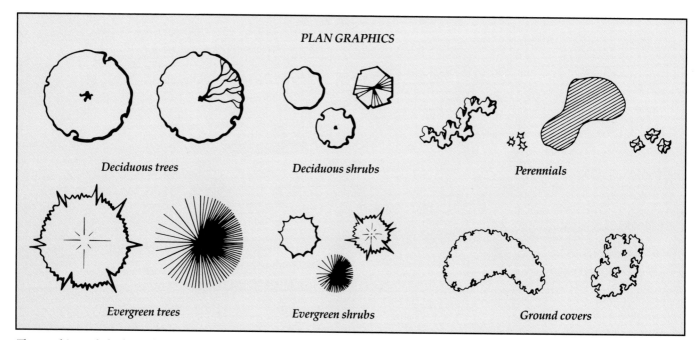

*The graphic symbols shown here are commonly used on professional landscape designs to indicate different types of plants. Sizes vary to indicate the plants' mature sizes.*

using a directional arrow, mark which way is north. Once your drawing is complete, have it photocopied so that the original is kept safe and clean while you experiment with the copies.

Now you're ready to design the new landscape for your property. If you're adapting a plan from this book, use a scale ruler to enlarge it to fit the same scale as your existing plot plan. If you're starting with blueprints, you won't need to redraw anything.

Lay the tracing-paper copy of your existing landscape over the blueprints or enlarged tracing of the landscape plan from the book, and see how good a fit you have. Place another piece of tracing paper on top of the two drawings (you can use small pieces of tape to keep the sheets aligned), and then begin to make adjustments to the layout, if necessary.

## Making the Fit: Adapting the Plan to Your Property

Most likely, any plan in this book won't fit your property exactly— almost, but not exactly. (The designs were created to fit typical properties of various sizes.) If your property varies from these sizes, that shouldn't be a major problem, because a few professional tricks will allow you to adapt the plans to a larger, smaller, or differently shaped yard. Here's how to do it: Tape a new sheet of tracing paper over both your present plot plan and the landscape design you wish to adapt. Trace only the permanent features and dimensions of your present yard onto the new sheet of paper. Then undo the tape, remove the tracing of the existing plot, and shift the new paper over the plan that you wish to adapt, tracing the design's prominent features in slightly different locations. The following are some examples of how to make specific adjustments.

## Adjusting for Different Lot Sizes and Shapes

Your property may be a bit longer, narrower, or larger than the average-sized properties for which these designs were created. If you intend to use one of these basic designs for a larger property, there are several

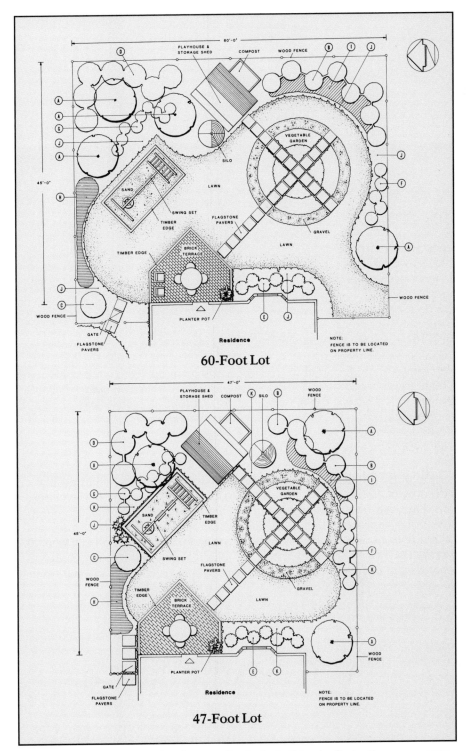

You can adapt a landscape plan for a smaller lot by judiciously eliminating one or more of a group of plants and rearranging other features to create a compact version of the original design. The plan pictured on top was created for a 60-foot-wide lot. The version pictured on the bottom shows how this was adapted to a 47-foot-wide lot by eliminating several trees, repositioning a few shrubs, and eliminating some lawn.

options available. Where the property line is farther to the left, keep the planting bed on the left the same size and simply redraw it along the edge of the property line, making up for the difference by in-

creasing the size of the lawn. It's more economical to widen the lawn area than to increase the number of shrubs. You can also make the planting bed slightly deeper, but not so deep that it's

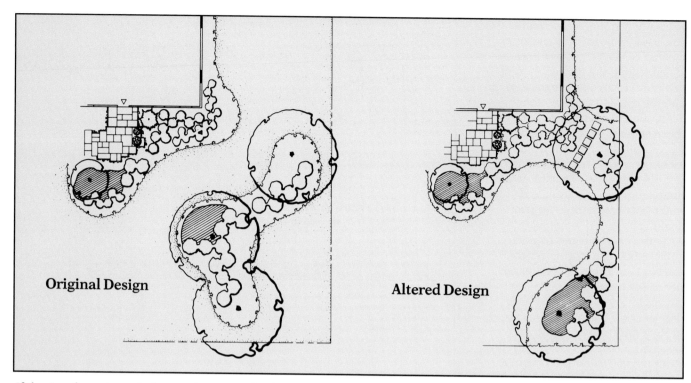

*If the size of your house is closer to the property border than is indicated on the plot plan, it is easy to adapt the design to fit your lot. The original design (left) employs three trees and an island bed to the side of the yard. The altered design (right) uses the same plants but rearranges them to fit the smaller space by eliminating one of the trees and some of the shrubs, and extending the groundcover bed into an appealing arc.*

hard to maintain or is out of scale with the rest of the design.

To use any of these designs on a much larger property, you may choose to keep the planting beds just about where they're shown in the plan and use a backdrop of tall evergreen trees for additional privacy. Moving a planting bed over to the left or right to accommodate a larger property often leaves a gap in the planting. Fill in this gap at a suitable point, such as where the bed curves around toward the house, by adding more plants of the same type; for example, plant five yews instead of three. Where even larger areas need to be filled in, repeat an entire group of plantings, which may include another tree of the same type, along with additional shrubs and more groundcovers and perennials.

A professional designer doesn't regard the lawn area as a catchall to solve leftover space, and neither should you. The size and shape of the lawns on these plans represent an important part of the overall design. The lawn acts as a sculptural element; it guides views and circulation around the property. Maintain

the shape of the lawn and its relationship with the rest of the plantings as much as possible when making adjustments in scale. This may mean enlarging island beds or including an additional tree or two to maintain balance on a larger property. Conversely, on a smaller property, you may wish to scale down the size of island beds and remove one or more trees from a group.

When you're reducing the size of a lawn, keep in mind that a turf area less than 6 to 8 feet wide serves little design purpose and is difficult to maintain. In such an instance, substitute a groundcover or paving for the lawn. Large trees and shrubs that border a lawn area will be out of proportion if the size of the lawn is greatly reduced. When this occurs, substitute smaller trees and shrubs in place of the larger ones to scale down that portion of the design. Conversely, increasing the size of the lawn significantly calls for larger trees and shrubs at the perimeter.

It's not difficult to adjust a larger design to a smaller piece of property. For instance, if the distance to the right side of the property line from the house is smaller than on

the plan, include only one tree with its underplantings where three are indicated, and make the lawn area smaller as necessary.

You can remove a shrub grouping entirely to reduce the size of a plan, or you can take out several plants from each group of shrubs and perennials along the width or depth of the property to adjust the design. Professional designers usually work with odd numbers of plants. You may see one specimen tree or a planting of three, five, or seven shrubs, but you'll rarely see two, four, or six of a particular plant. When making adjustments, follow professional design techniques and expand or contract the planting by working with odd numbers.

## Adjusting for a Different House Layout

Are you saying, "I like the design, but my house has a wing on the other side"? Or perhaps, "The sliding doors from the dining room face the other direction"? Most differences in house layout can easily be accommodated to your design using the tracing-paper technique.

If your house is a mirror image of

one shown here, the solution is simple: Trace the plot plan and then flip the paper over. *Voilá!* You have an instant landscape plan.

Whenever an adjustment is made for a different house layout, remember that the professional designer used certain principles when creating the landscape plan. Any adjustments you make must be done with those principles in mind. Any changes to one side will need balancing changes on the other side. Remember, too, that balance doesn't necessarily mean symmetry. If you're not sure how to accomplish this, you may want to consult a professional designer.

*This attractive stone retaining wall creates two flat areas where the ground once sloped. The wall also provides year-round interest and a perfect backdrop for displaying flowers and foliage.*

## Adjusting Plans to a Sloped Property

The landscapes illustrated in Chapters 3 and 4 were created for relatively flat pieces of property or for properties with a slight slope away from the house. If your property is more sloped, you can adjust many of these plans to fit, either by re-grading or by working with the existing terrain and adding a series of steps and landings or even retaining walls. A change of grade involves more than just aesthetics. Rather than a professional designer, you may require an engineer or licensed contractor to ensure that changing the grade doesn't create drainage problems.

Retaining walls are often used by professional designers to create several flat levels out of steeply sloped ground. The walls are not only functional, but also attractive. Build walls out of landscape timbers, bricks, stones, or another material that matches your home's architecture. You can regrade and incorporate retaining walls into many of the designs shown here using the same basic plot plan. If the retaining wall intersects a walkway, include steps and perhaps a landing in the walk to accommodate the change in levels. When planning a retaining wall, include drainage pipes at the base of the wall to prevent water buildup behind the wall.

## Adjusting for Grading and Drainage

Sometimes it seems that the grass really is greener on the other side. People who live where the land is flat find it dull and uninteresting, and often they go out of their way to create height and contours in the garden. People who live on a sloped property often try to flatten it out so they can play volleyball or get up the driveway more easily when it's covered with ice and snow.

Even a property that seems flat may not really be perfectly flat. Almost every property has some grade (slope) or dips and rises. The "grade" of a property shouldn't be confused with "grading," which is the term used to describe changing the existing slope. You should assess the variations in grade on your property and consider any necessary or desired grade changes before finalizing your landscape design.

Grading needs may be minimal or extensive. You may need to flatten an area for a patio or a ground-level deck. Your lawn may need grading so that it slopes evenly away from the house toward the street. Some plans call for adding mounds of earth, known as berms, for effectively screening a view or adding interesting height to an otherwise flat property. Changes of grade can also be used to separate one activity area of the landscape from another.

The grade shouldn't be changed around the drip line of a large tree, because this can either expose or bury the roots, eventually killing the tree. If it becomes necessary to raise the grade around a tree, construct a well around it to avoid burying the roots.

## Drainage Considerations

Grading and drainage are interdependent. It's best to grade your property so that water drains away from structures and doesn't collect in beds, borders, and paved areas. Proper grading prevents having to pump water out of the basement after heavy rains. It eliminates low areas where water and snow collect instead of draining away properly. Water should drain quickly from paved areas so that the pavement doesn't become an icy hazard or remain unusable for hours after a rainstorm.

Paved areas should maintain a minimum pitch of ⅛ inch per foot, but ¼ inch is better. A patio that's located next to the house should slope away slightly from the structure. If the patio is located in a lower part of the landscape where water can't run off because a wall or higher ground surrounds the paving, then you'll need drains and drain pipes to channel water away. Discuss the matter with a professional designer to ensure a practical and economical solution.

It's wise to know how well your soil drains before you plan any grade changes. You can use a simple method that professionals employ for testing drainage: Dig a hole 2 feet deep by any width; you can dig

*Before: A tumbledown wall and uneven steps create an unsightly hazard in this landscape which is ready for remodeling and renovation.*

*After: The new design replaces steep steps with a more gradual climb, and incorporates dwarf evergreens, spreading perennials and groundcovers to weave around the moss rocks for a naturalistic feel.*

a narrow hole with a posthole digger if the soil is hard. Fill the hole with water and let it drain for a day, then fill it again. If it's empty or less than one-third full the following day, there is no drainage problem. If it's still two-thirds or more full, the drainage problem is severe, and you may need to install drainage pipes or tiles. If the hole is between one-third and two-thirds full, you may be able to correct the drainage problem by amending the soil.

Consider your soil structure. Will changing the grade expose areas with poor soil and bury good topsoil? It may be necessary to change the grade using a two-step process: You may have to remove the topsoil and hold it in reserve, do the grading, and then replace the topsoil. You may also need to purchase soil to complete a grading project—a decision that will affect your budget. Soil is expensive, so try to fill in low areas of your property by moving soil from a higher level. Any soil that you purchase should be as close as possible in texture and composi-

tion to the existing soil. Placing a fast-draining soil over a heavy, poor-draining soil causes a subsurface drainage problem that may drown the plants growing above. Removing trees and shrubs when you change the grade may also alter the drainage pattern, sometimes for the better, sometimes not.

Consultation with utility companies may be necessary to determine the location of underground pipes and cables. Proposed changes in grade may be impossible if the pipes and cables will be exposed or if access to them or their meters will be blocked.

You shouldn't just move soil around the garden or pave large areas without first thinking of the consequences. Before attempting any major changes in grade or before paving large areas near the house, consult a professional to ensure that your plan won't cause drainage problems. He or she can help you determine whether some type of drainage tiles or pipes need to be installed, or how to

change the grade to avoid potential problems.

If your property is relatively flat and the soil is naturally fast draining, you needn't be too concerned about drainage; follow the principles outlined for changing grade to ensure that any new structures or paved areas have proper drainage. On the other hand, if you have heavy soil, consult a professional regarding the installation of drainage pipes.

## Installing the Landscape

Whether you plant the shrubs and trees and construct the walkways and the deck or patio yourself, or hire a contractor to do all or part of the work, there are several things you should consider:

### Construction Regulations

Many communities have building codes that may affect how you install your landscape. City building and planning departments create these rules for good reasons, primarily to ensure the safety of current and subsequent owners,

*Balled-and-burlapped shrubs are easy to plant. Top left: Dig a hole larger and wider than the rootball. Improve the backfill by mixing in peat or compost, returning some soil to the bottom of the hole. Top right: Place the plant in the hole so it is level with the soil surface. Bottom left: Fold back the burlap, fill the hole partway and water. Bottom right: Fill the hole to the top, gently press the soil in place, then form a ring of soil over the rootball to hold water.*

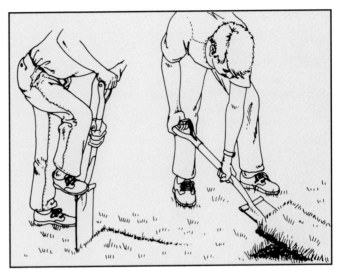

*When starting a new planting bed where lawn is growing, first strip off the sod with a spade, then turn over the soil. This prevents the grass from returning as weeds.*

and to maintain the community's attractive appearance. It's your responsibility to find out which, if any, regulations govern your landscape plans.

If you're planning to install new plants only, you probably won't need a permit, although the height of shrubs, walls, and fences at the property line may be restricted in some situations. Permanent structures and home improvements, such as decks, patios, and retaining walls, may require building permits. The city will require proof of proper engineering, and, in most cases, it may demand that such structures be a certain distance from the property line. Swimming pools almost always require a fence enclosure to prevent small children from accidentally wandering into the area.

## Transferring Your Plan

Once you've cleared the area to be landscaped, transfer your plan to your property. Using a measuring tape, accurately measure the location of all new walkways, structures, and plants. Place markers to indicate areas of major construction, such as a deck, a pool, or walkways. Mark the sites of major trees and the outline of planting beds and borders. You can use wood or metal stakes and run strings between them to show clearly where everything will be located. A garden hose or a clothesline works well to outline beds and borders.

Stand on the site of the proposed deck and double-check the location and the views. Note if trees are properly located. Walk from the side of the house to the various doors to make sure the walkways are in the most logical place. Walk out to the gate or side yard and see what a first-time visitor will see. Go inside and look at your landscape from indoors. When you're pleased with all aspects of the design, then you can start to put your plan into action.

## Planting Your Landscape

In most cases, thorough soil preparation before planting is essential for the ongoing health of plants. The best way to start is with a soil test. Contact your local county extension service or a private soil-testing laboratory. Along with the results, you'll get detailed recommendations on how to improve your soil. These will most likely indicate adding organic matter, such as composted fir bark or sawdust. Spread 2 or 3 inches of the organic material over the soil where you've located the planting beds, and till it in. Additional fertilizer, and perhaps lime or sulfur to adjust the soil pH, may also be recommended.

## Removing Lawn

There are several ways to remove an existing lawn where new beds and borders, walkways, or a patio will go. The lawn can be stripped away just below the roots with a spade, or you can rent a power sod cutter. Sod that's stripped off can be saved and transplanted where it's needed. If you have no need for the sod, use it as fill or add it to the compost pile. When building a ground-level deck,

don't bother removing the lawn under it, because the grass will soon die from lack of light. Lawns can also be killed with an herbicide such as glyphosate, but be careful not to spray the chemical accidentally on desirable plants, or you'll kill them, too.

If you're removing an existing lawn and installing a new one in the same area, take advantage of the situation and improve the soil. Both seeded and sodded lawns will be healthier and will need less care for years to come if the soil has been amended. Till organic matter into the soil and level the ground. Roll the surface after seeding or sodding. Keep the newly planted lawn moist until it's well established.

### Planting Trees and Shrubs

Trees and shrubs are available as dormant bare-root, balled-and-burlapped (B&B), or container-grown plants. Both bare-root and B&B plants are grown in native soil in nursery fields. Bare-roots are dug while they're dormant, and the soil is washed off. Since they're quite perishable, they should be planted promptly. B&B plants are similarly field-grown and dug up, but the soil surrounding the root ball is retained and wrapped with burlap or a synthetic fabric. B&B plants can survive for weeks before planting, but it's wise to keep them shaded and moist. Bare-root plants are best planted in late winter, and B&B plants in early spring or fall, soon after they're dug up.

Container-grown plants can be installed anytime without suffering transplant shock, since their root systems are completely intact. Before removing a plant from its container, check to see if the soil is moist. If not, water the plant thoroughly and allow the soil to drain. When it's moist—not dry or soggy—it's much easier to handle and less prone to fall apart. Hold the plant upside down or lay it sideways on the ground, and gently let it fall or slide out of the container. Set the plant in the hole and check its height. To allow for soil settling, make sure the plant is slightly higher than it was in the container. If the roots are matted or circling, loosen them—heading them outward—before refilling the hole. Backfill halfway, apply water, then finish backfilling.

Newly planted trees and shrubs can suffer greatly from lack of water, since they haven't yet rooted into the surrounding soil. To help retain

*A handy do-it-yourselfer can put down a sod lawn. A: Unstack sod and keep it shaded and moist until you need it. B: Begin by laying the sod along the longest straight edge of the lawn space, butting the ends together. C: Lay subsequent rows in a staggered bricklike pattern, using a board to support your weight so the sod pieces will stay in place. D: Lastly, go over the sod with a roller to press the roots into the soil.*

water and direct it to roots, make a ring of raised soil around the plant and flood the basin periodically with water. After planting, apply an organic mulch, such as wood chips, over the soil to keep it moist and weed-free.

## Planting Groundcovers and Lawns

Many groundcovers are sold in flats or packs, as are most flowering annuals. Space them uniformly— usually five pachysandra, three English ivy, or three ajuga plants for every square foot. For quicker coverage, plant closer together; to save money, plant farther apart, although the plants will take longer to fill in. Apply mulch to keep the planting weed-free until the groundcover fills in.

Start a new lawn with either seeds or sod. A seeded lawn costs less, but requires more attention until it gets established. If the lawn area is greater than about 1,500 square feet, the savings gained by using seeds instead of sod are substantial. Sod costs more initially, but looks great right away. If the lawn is relatively small, the difference in actual cost is small.

The most important decision for you to make about a lawn is which type of grass to plant. Consult a knowledgeable nursery staff or your county extension agent about the best grass species and cultivars for your climate. Usually a mixture of several types is best, because a mix resists disease better than a single type.

You can install sod yourself or have it done professionally. Sod comes in several standard widths based on the size of the cutting tool, but the thickness should be between ½ and 1 inch—thicker pieces may not establish well. Sod often comes stacked or rolled, but it shouldn't be kept this way for more than 24 hours, because heat buildup can injure the grass. After delivery, unroll or unstack the pieces and lay them in the shade if you can't plant them immediately. Be sure to keep them moist.

Prepare the soil by tilling in organic matter. Rake it smooth and level, and water before planting the sod. Begin by installing the sod along the longest edge of the area to

be sodded. Lay the pieces in a staggered, bricklike pattern, butting the ends together. Use a serrated knife to cut pieces to fit curves. As you work, it's best to walk on a board laid across the sod to prevent the pieces from slipping.

Once the sod is laid, roll it at right angles with a heavy roller to press the roots into the soil. New sod requires watering several times a week for the first month or two. You can mow as soon as the lawn needs it, but don't fertilize until the next season.

The best time to sow seeds is in early spring or fall; fall sowing is usually more successful in any climate. You can sow successfully in winter in some warm climates, and you can probably get away with it in summer in some cool climates if you water adequately. Prepare the soil as described above, then spread the seeds evenly across the soil using a drop spreader. Divide the total amount of seeds needed by half, and spread them by walking across the area twice, making the second pass at right angles to the first. (The rate of seeding—number of pounds of seeds per 100 square feet—varies with grass type.) Roll the soil to press the seeds into the soil. Using a light mist that won't wash away the seeds, water every day to keep the soil surface moist until the seeds germinate—about 10 days. Continue watering regularly until the grass is established.

## Hiring a Landscape Contractor

The virtue of the plans offered in this book is that you can enjoy the benefits of a professional design without paying what you would for custom work. Many handy do-it-yourselfers can easily manage the variety of tasks required to install a landscape; others may wish to hire a landscape contractor to carry out some or all of the installation. For example, you may wish to do the planting and contract the brickwork or decking, or vice versa. A landscape contractor isn't, by definition, a designer. A contractor knows how to follow blueprints, plant trees and shrubs, build retaining walls, and the like. Rarely are landscape contractors skilled landscape designers, although they may offer to design a

*Be sure to provide yourself with a place to sit and enjoy your new easy-care garden, because if you design it right you'll have a lot more free time on the weekends.*

landscape. They may be able to purchase the landscape plants at a reduced cost to you if you hire them to install the landscape, thus offsetting some of the cost of their work.

Ask your friends and neighbors for recommendations for a contractor, and ask to see examples of their work. Ask each prospective contractor for cost and scheduling estimates. Don't neglect to compare lists of materials and their relative quality when making your choice. Once you've decided on an individual, write out a contract that specifies work and payment schedules. Under no circumstances should you post a construction bond for a contractor. Keep copies of all plans, building permits, certificates of occupancy, and inspections after the work is completed; you'll need them when you sell the house.

When your landscape is finished, the property will have a beautiful look that you and your family will enjoy for years to come. Your new easy-care landscape will improve your outdoor living environment the day it's completed, and the initial investment will more than pay for itself over the years by continuing to add to the increasing value of your home.

# CHAPTER 6

# Plans For Garden Structures & Decks

Many of the backyard landscapes in Chapter 4 include garden structures and decks that beautifully complete the yard. More detailed illustrations are shown on the following pages. Plans for these structures and decks are available through Timeless Designs and Home Planners, Inc.

In addition to the structures and decks shown, Home Planners has a full complement of other outdoor enhancements available. A useful book, *Deck Planner*, contains 25 decks—each of which has complete construction drawings available—in many sizes and styles. *Creative Plans For Yard & Garden Structures* is another Home Planners book which contains 42 gazebos, sheds, playhouses, studios and cottages, cabanas, trellises, arbors and other outdoor structures. See pages 158-159 for information about ordering these books.

Timeless Designs publishes books and plans for a wide variety of products made from wood. These products range from Gazebos, Backyard Structures, Cupolas and Bridges, to children's toys such as Wagons, Sleighs, Rocking Horses and other wooden objects. The designs on the following pages provide interesting and practical ways to add exciting amenities to your favorite backyard plan.

For more information on obtaining construction drawings for the plans shown—or for information on the full line of plan books available—call, write or FAX:

Timeless Designs
P.O. Box 676
Whitewater, WI 53190
**TOLL FREE 1-800-765-0176**
**FAX 414-473-6112**

**Mourning Dove Feeder**
Type: Open feeder
Size: 11″ x 11″
Height: 14″

**Warbler Birdhouse**
Type: Enclosed house
Size: 29″ x 29″
Height: 42″

**Bluebird Feeder**
Type: Feeder with glass
Size: 10″ x 10″
Height: 11″

**Fairfax Swing**
Layout: Rectangular shape
Size: 3′ 6″ x 5′ 8″
Height: 8′ 2″ ground to top

**Greenwood Arbor**
Layout: Rectangular shape
Size: 12′ x 10′
Height: 9′ ground to top

# Garden Structures

The blueprint package for the garden structures shown here contains everything you need for planning and building the structure of your choice. Included is information such as floor plans, elevations, framing plans, wall sections, foundation and joist details, a materials list and other details. Some of the more complicated structures will have several sheets to thoroughly explain how it will go together. The simpler structures have fewer sheets.

To help you further understand the process of building an outdoor structure, we also offer a separate package— **Gazebo Construction Details**— for $14.95. This package outlines general information for constructing outdoor enhancements. Included are numerous illustrations, an explanation of building terms, and general tips and hints to make your building project progress smoothly. When you buy the **Complete Construction Package,** you will receive blueprints for the structure of your choice as well as a set of Gazebo Construction Details for one low price.

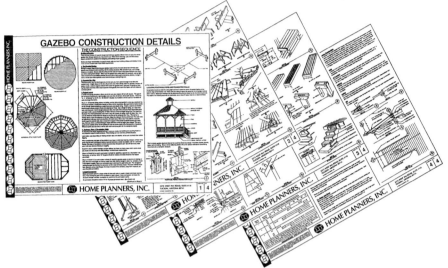

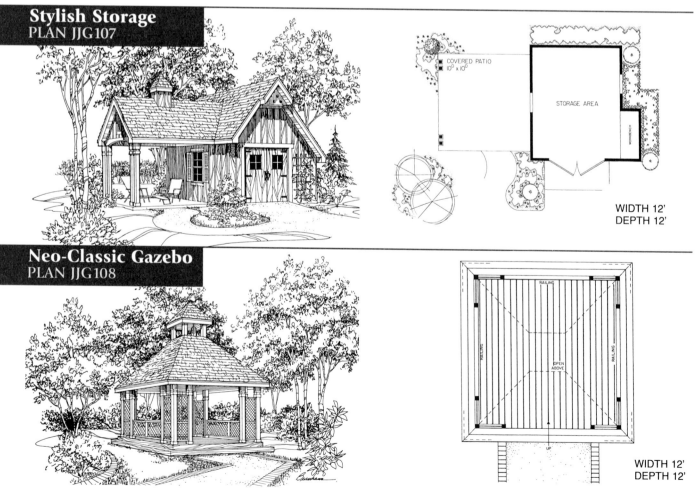

## Stylish Storage
### PLAN JJG 107

WIDTH 12'
DEPTH 12'

## Neo-Classic Gazebo
### PLAN JJG 108

WIDTH 12'
DEPTH 12'

# American Classic
## PLAN JJG215

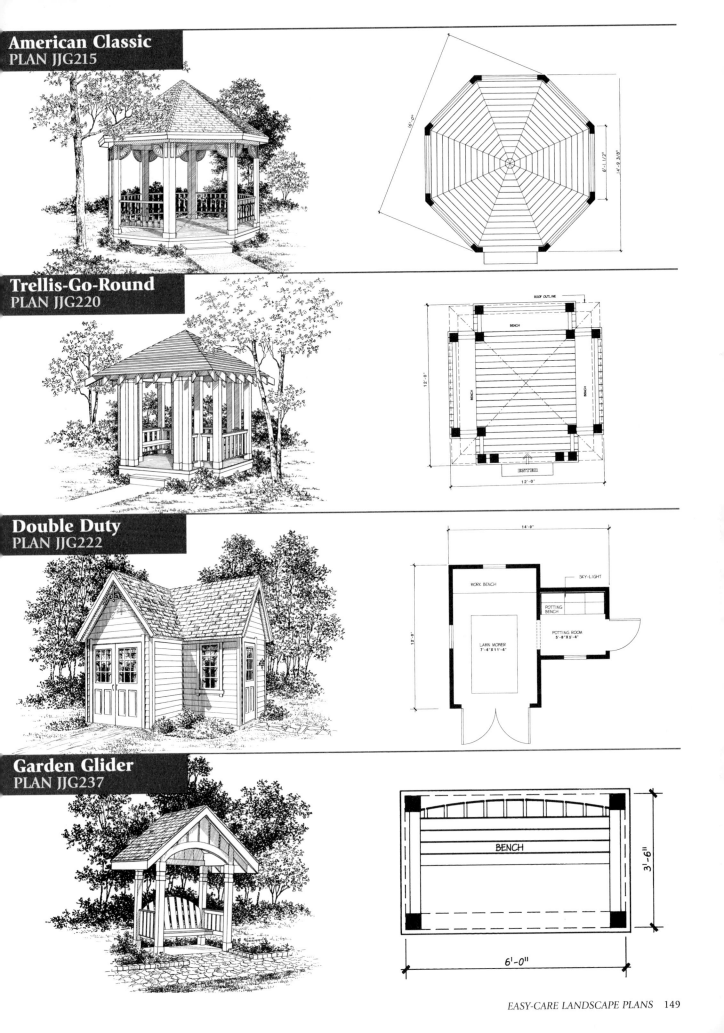

16'-0"

14'-9 3/8"

6'-1 1/2"

# Trellis-Go-Round
## PLAN JJG220

ROOF OUTLINE

BENCH

BENCH

BENCH

12'-0"

12'-0"

REGISTER

# Double Duty
## PLAN JJG222

14'-0"

WORK BENCH

SKY-LIGHT

POTTING BENCH

POTTING ROOM
5'-8" X 5'-4"

LAWN MOWER
7'-4" X 11'-4"

12'-0"

# Garden Glider
## PLAN JJG237

BENCH

3'-6"

6'-0"

# Deck Plans

The plans and details for building decks are carefully prepared in an easy-to-understand format that will guide you through every stage of your deck-building project. The deck blueprint package contains four sheets outlining information pertinent to the specific deck plan you have chosen. The sheets include a deck plan frontal sheet showing an artist's line drawing of the deck, deck framing and floor plans, a materials list, and deck elevations.

A separate package—**Deck Construction Details**—provides the how-to data for building any deck, including instructions for adaptations and conversions. It is available for $14.95 and contains layout examples, details for ledgers and beams, schedules and charts, handrail and stair details and much more. Order the **Complete Construction Package** and you'll receive a set of deck plans of your choice plus the Deck Construction Details, all at one low price.

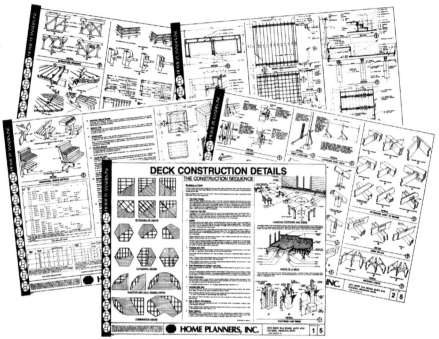

## Deck Plan JJD115

## Deck Plan JJD118

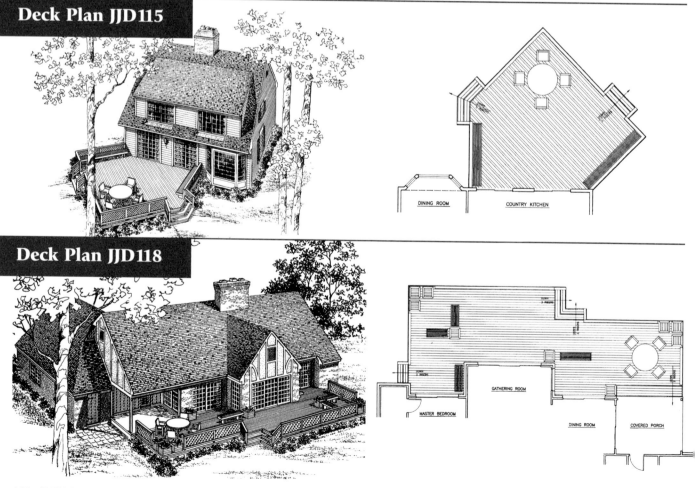

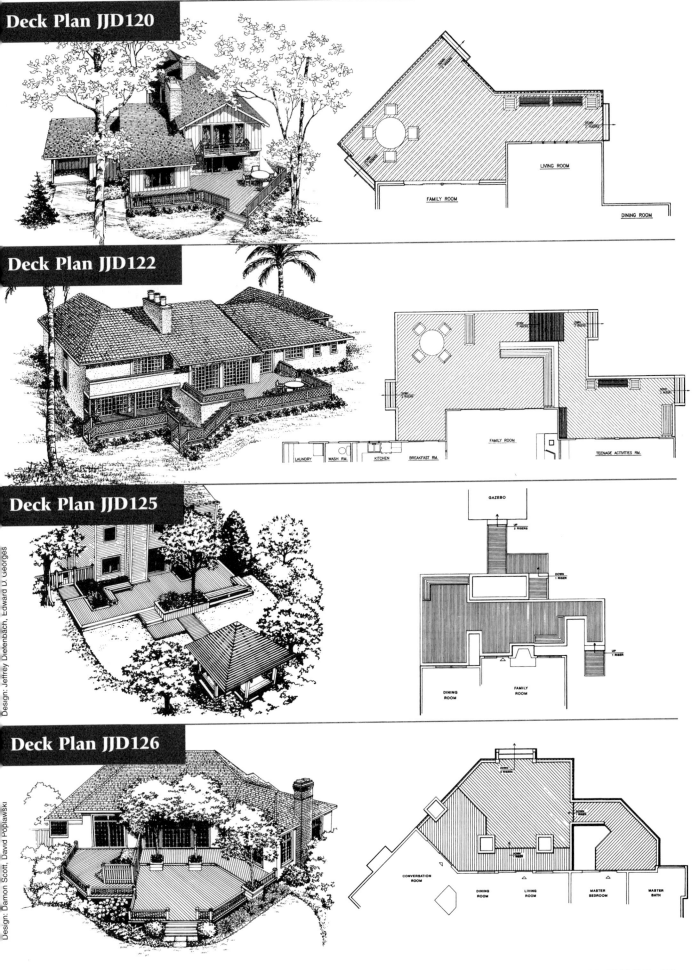

# Deck Plan JJD120

FAMILY ROOM

LIVING ROOM

DINING ROOM

# Deck Plan JJD122

LAUNDRY  WASH RM.  KITCHEN  BREAKFAST RM.  FAMILY ROOM  TEENAGE ACTIVITIES RM.

# Deck Plan JJD125

GAZEBO

UP
2 RISERS

DOWN
1 RISER

UP
1 RISER

DINING
ROOM

FAMILY
ROOM

Design: Jeffrey Diefenbach, Edward D. Georges

# Deck Plan JJD126

CONVERSATION
ROOM

DINING
ROOM

LIVING
ROOM

MASTER
BEDROOM

MASTER
BATH

Design: Damon Scott, David Poplawski

# Garden Structures Price Schedule and Index

## Garden Structures Price Schedule

Yard and Garden Structures

| Price Group | GD1 | GD2 | GD3 | GD4 | GD5 | GD6 |
|---|---|---|---|---|---|---|
| 1 Set Custom Plans | $20 | $30 | $40 | $50 | $75 | $85 |

Additional Identical Sets . . . . . . . . . . . . . . . . . . . . . . . . $10 each
Reverse Sets (mirror image). . . . . . . . . . . . . . . . . . . . . $10 each

Gazebo Construction Details
1 set Generic Gazebo Construction Details . . . . . . . . $14.95 each

Complete Construction Package

| Price Group | GD1 | GD2 | GD3 | GD4 | GD5 | GD6 |
|---|---|---|---|---|---|---|
| 1 Set Custom Plans, plus 1 Set Gazebo Construction Details | $30 | $40 | $50 | $60 | $85 | $95 |

# Deck Plans Price Schedule and Index

## Deck Plans Price Schedule

Custom Deck Plans

| Price Group | Q | R | S |
|---|---|---|---|
| 1 Set Custom Plans | $25 | $30 | $35 |

Additional Identical Sets . . . . . . . . . . . . . . . . . . . . . . . . $10 each
Reverse Sets (mirror image) . . . . . . . . . . . . . . . . . . . . . $10 each

Standard Deck Details
1 set Generic Gazebo Construction Details           $14.95 each

Complete Deck Building Package

| Price Group | Q | R | S |
|---|---|---|---|
| 1 Set Custom Plans, plus 1 Set Standard Deck Details | $35 | $40 | $45 |

**TO ORDER:** Find the Plan number in the Plans Index (opposite). Consult the Price Schedule (opposite) to determine the price of your plan, adding any additional or reverse sets you desire. Or specify the Complete Construction Package, which contains 1 set of Custom Plans of your choice, plus 1 set of Construction Details. Complete the order form on this page and mail with your check or money order. Please include the correct postage and handling fees. If you prefer, you can also use a credit card and call our toll-free number, 1-800-521-6797, to place your order.

### Our Service Policy
We try to process and ship every order from our office within 48 hours. For this reason, we won't send a formal notice acknowledging receipt of your order.

### Our Exchange Policy
Because we produce and ship plans in response to individual orders, we cannot honor requests for refunds. However, you can exchange your entire order of blueprints, including a single set if you order just one, for a set of another design. All exchanges carry an additional fee of $15.00 plus $8.00 postage and handling if they're sent Regular Service; $12.00 via 2nd Day Air; $22.00 via Next Day Air.

### About Reverse Blueprints
If you want to install your structure in reverse of the plan as shown, we will include an extra set of blueprints with the images reversed for an additional fee of $10.00. Although callouts and lettering appear backward, reverses will prove useful as a visual aid if you decide to flop the plan.

### How Many Blueprints Do You Need?
To study your favorite design, one set of blueprints may be sufficient. On the other hand, if you plan to use contractors or subcontractors to complete the project, you will probably need more sets. Use the checklist below to estimate the number of sets you'll need.

_____ Owner
_____ Contractor or Subcontractor
_____ Building Materials Supplier
_____ Lender or Mortgage Source, if applicable
_____ Community Building Department for Permits
            (sometimes requires 2 sets)
_____ Subdivision Committee, if any
_____ Total Number of Sets

**Blueprint Hotline**
**Call Toll Free 1-800-521-6797.** We try to process and ship every order within 48 hours. When you order by phone, please be prepared to give us the Order Form Key Number shown in the box at the bottom of the Order Form.

**By FAX:** Copy the order form at right and send on our FAX line: 1-800-224-6699 or 1-520-297-9937.

### Canadian Customers
**Order Toll Free 1-800-561-4169**
For faster service and plans that are modified for building in Canada, customers may now call in orders directly to our Canadian supplier of plans and charge the purchase to a charge card. Or, you may complete the order form at right, adding 40% to all prices and mail in Canadian funds to:       **The Plan Centre**
                                20 Cedar Street North
                                Kitchener, Ontario N2H 2W8

**By FAX:** Copy the Order Form at right and send it via our Canadian FAX line: 1-519-743-1282.

## BLUEPRINTS ARE NOT RETURNABLE

**HOME PLANNERS, INC.**
**3275 WEST INA ROAD, SUITE 110**
**TUCSON, ARIZONA 85741**

Please rush me the following:

| | | |
|---|---|---|
| _____ Set(s) of Custom Plan _____ | | |
| (See Index and Price Schedule) | $ _____ | |
| _____ Additional identical blueprints in | | |
| same order at $10 per set. | $ _____ | |
| _____ Reverse blueprints at $10 per set. | $ _____ | |
| _____ Sets of Construction Details at | | |
| $14.95 per set. | $ _____ | |
| _____ Sets of Complete Construction Package (Best Buy!) | | |
| Includes Custom Plan _____ | | |
| Plus Construction Details | $ _____ | |

**POSTAGE AND HANDLING**

| Carrier Delivery (Requires street address—No P.O Boxes) | | |
|---|---|---|
| • Regular Service (Allow 4-6 days delivery) | $ 8.00 | $ _____ |
| • 2nd Day Air (Allow 2-3 days delivery) | $12.00 | $ _____ |
| • Next Day Air (Allow 1 day delivery) | $22.00 | $ _____ |
| Certified Mail (requires signature) If no street address available. (Allow 4-6 days delivery) | $10.00 | $ _____ |
| Overseas Delivery | Phone, FAX or Mail for Quote | |

*NOTE: All delivery times are from date blueprint package is shipped.*

| | |
|---|---|
| POSTAGE (from box above) | $ _____ |
| SUB-TOTAL | $ _____ |
| SALES TAX (Arizona residents add 5% sales tax; Michigan residents add 6% sales tax.) | $ _____ |
| TOTAL (Sub-total and Tax) | $ _____ |

YOUR ADDRESS (please print)

Name _____

Street _____

City _____ State _____ ZIP _____

Daytime telephone number    (_____) _____

FOR CREDIT CARD ORDERS ONLY
Please fill in the information below:

Credit card number _____

Exp. Date: Month/Year _____

Check One:    ☐ Visa   ☐ MasterCard   ☐ Discover Card

Signature _____

## ORDER TOLL FREE
## 1-800-521-6797
## OR 1-520-297-8200

Order Form Key
TB38BP

# Ordering Landscape Plans

## The Landscape Blueprint Package

The Landscape Blueprint Package available from Home Planners includes all the necessary information you need to lay out and install the landscape design of your choice. Professionally designed and prepared with attention to detail, these clear, easy-to-follow plans offer everything from a precise plot plan and regionalized plant and materials list to helpful sheets on installing your landscape and determining the mature size of your plants. These plans, together with the information in Chapter 5 on adapting the design to your lot, will help you achieve professional-looking results, adding value and enjoyment to your property for years to come.

Each set of blueprints is a full 18" x 24" in size with clear, complete instructions and easy-to-read type. Consisting of six detailed sheets, these plans show how all plants and materials are put together to form an exciting landscape for your home

**Frontal Sheet.** *This artist's line sketch shows a typical house and all the elements of the finished landscape when plants are at or near maturity. This will give you a visual image or "picture" of the design and what you might expect your property to look like when fully landscaped.*

**Plan View.** *Drawn at 1/8" equals 1'-0", this is an aerial view of the property showing the exact placement of all landscape elements, including symbols and callouts for flowers, shrubs, ground covers, walkways, walls, gates, and other garden amenities. This sheet is the key to the design and shows you the contour, spacing, flow, and balance of all the elements in the design, as well as providing an exact "map" for laying out your property.*

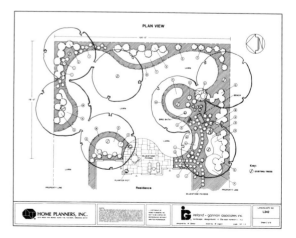

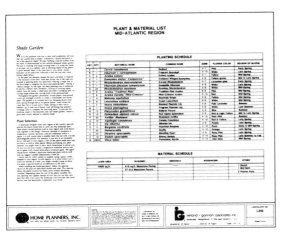

**Regionalized Plan & Materials List.** *Keyed to the Plan View sheet, this page lists all of the plants and materials necessary to execute the design. It gives the quantity, botanical name, common name, flower color, season of bloom, and hardiness zones for each plant specified, as well as the amount and type of materials for all driveways, walks, walls, gates, and other structures. This becomes your "shopping list" for dealing with contractors or buying the plants and materials yourself. Most importantly, the plants shown on this page have been chosen by a team of professional horticulturalists for their adaptability, availability, and performance in your specific part of the country.*

**Planting and Maintaining Your Landscape.** *This valuable sheet gives handy information and illustrations on purchasing plant materials, preparing your site, and caring for your landscape after installation. Includes quick, helpful advice on planting trees, shrubs and ground covers, staking trees, establishing a lawn, watering, weed control, and pruning.*

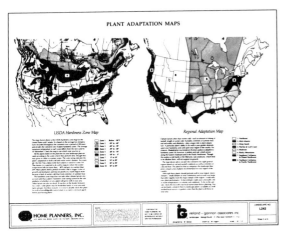

**Zone Maps.** *These two informative maps offer detailed information to help you better select and judge the performance of your plants. Map One is a United States Department of Agriculture Hardiness Zone Map that shows the average low temperatures by zones in various parts of the United States and Canada. The "Zone" listing for plants on Sheet 3 of your Plant and Materials List is keyed to this map. Map Two is a Regional Adaptation Map which takes into account other factors beyond low temperatures, such as rainfall, humidity, extremes of temperature, and soil acidity or alkalinity. Both maps are key to plant adaptability and are used for the selection of landscape plants for your plans.*

**Plant Size & Description Guide.** *Because you may have trouble visualizing certain plants, this handy regionalized guide provides a scale and silhouettes to help you determine the final height and shape of various trees and shrubs in your landscape plan. It also provides a quick means of choosing alternate plants appropriate to your region in case you do not wish to install a certain tree or shrub, or if you cannot find the plant at local nurseries.*

*To order, see page 157.*

# Plans Price Schedule and Index

To order your plans, simply find the Plan Number of the design of your choice in the Plans Index below. Consult the Price Schedule at right to determine the price of your plans, choosing the 1-, 3-, or 6-set package and any additional or reverse sets you desire. To make sure your Plant and Materials List contains the best selection for your area, refer to the Regional Order Map below and specify the region in which you reside. Fill out the Order Coupon on the opposite page and mail it to us for prompt fulfillment or call our Toll-Free Order Hotline for even faster service.

## Landscape Plans Price Schedule

| Price Group | W | X | Y | Z |
|---|---|---|---|---|
| 1 set | $25 | $35 | $45 | $55 |
| 3 sets | $40 | $50 | $60 | $70 |
| 6 sets | $55 | $65 | $75 | $85 |

Additional Identical Sets . . . . . . . . . . . . . . .$10 each
Reverse Sets (Mirror Image)  . . . . . . . . . . .$10 each

## Front Yard Designs

| Landscape Plans | Page | Price | Available For Regions: |
|---|---|---|---|
| L200 | 76 | X | 1-3,5,6 & 8 |
| L202 | 78 | X | 1-3,5,6 & 8 |
| L280 | 52 | X | ALL |
| L281 | 54 | Y | ALL |
| L282 | 56 | X | ALL |
| L283 | 58 | X | ALL |
| L284 | 60 | Y | ALL |
| L285 | 62 | Z | ALL |
| L286 | 64 | Z | ALL |
| L287 | 66 | Z | ALL |
| L288 | 68 | Z | ALL |
| L289 | 70 | Z | ALL |
| L290 | 72 | Y | ALL |
| L291 | 74 | Y | ALL |
| L292 | 80 | X | ALL |
| L293 | 82 | Y | ALL |
| L294 | 84 | Y | ALL |
| L295 | 86 | Y | ALL |

## Backyard Designs

| Landscape Plans | Page | Price | Available For Regions: |
|---|---|---|---|
| L241 | 114 | Y | ALL |
| L242 | 94 | Y | ALL |
| L245 | 122 | Y | ALL |
| L248 | 112 | Z | ALL |
| L258 | 108 | Z | 1-3,5,6 & 8 |
| L266 | 100 | Y | ALL |
| L267 | 126 | Z | ALL |
| L268 | 104 | Y | ALL |
| L275 | 124 | Z | ALL |
| L277 | 128 | W | ALL |
| L296 | 90 | Z | 1-6 & 8 |
| L297 | 96 | Z | 1-6 & 8 |
| L298 | 92 | Y | 1-3,5,6 & 8 |
| L300 | 102 | Y | ALL |
| L301 | 106 | Z | ALL |
| L302 | 110 | Z | ALL |
| L303 | 116 | Z | ALL |
| L304 | 118 | Z | ALL |
| L305 | 120 | Y | ALL |
| L306 | 130 | W | ALL |
| L307 | 132 | X | ALL |
| L308 | 134 | X | ALL |

## Regional Order Map

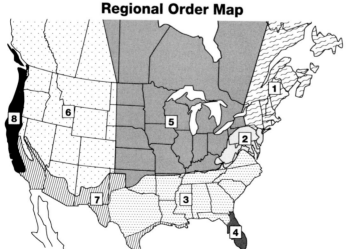

Region 1 Northeast
Region 2 Mid-Atlantic
Region 3 Deep South
Region 4 Florida & Gulf Coast
Region 5 Midwest
Region 6 Rocky Mountains
Region 7 Southern California
      & Desert Southwest
Region 8 Northern California
      & Pacific Northwest

**TO ORDER:** Just clip the accompanying order blank and mail with your check or money order. If you prefer, you can also use a credit card. If time is of essence, call us Toll-Free at 1-800-521-6797 on our Blueprint Hotline. We try to process and ship every order within 48 hours. Because of this quick turnaround, we won't send a formal notice acknowledging receipt of your order. If you use the coupon, please include the correct postage and handling charges.

## Our Exchange Policy
Because we produce and ship plans in response to individual orders, we cannot honor requests for refunds. However, you can exchange your entire order of blueprints, including a single set if you order just one, for a set of another landscape design. All exchanges carry an additional fee of $15.00 plus $8.00 for postage and handling if they're sent via surface mail; $10.00 for priority air mail.

## About Reverse Blueprints
If you want to install your landscape in reverse of the plan as shown, we will include an extra set of blueprints with the Frontal Sheet and Plan View reversed for an additional fee of $10.00. Although callouts and lettering appear backward, reverses will prove useful as a visual aid if you decide to flop the plan.

## How Many Blueprints Do You Need?
To study your favorite landscape design or make alterations of the plan to fit your site, one set of blueprints may be sufficient. On the other hand, if you plan to install the landscape yourself using subcontractors or have a general contractor do the work for you, you will probably need more sets. Because you save money on 3-set or 6-set packages, you should consider ordering all the sets at one time. Use the checklist below to estimate the number of sets you'll need:

## Blueprint Checklist
_____ Owner
_____ Contractor or Subcontractor
_____ Nursery or Plant Materials Supplier
_____ Building Materials Supplier
_____ Lender or Mortgage Source, if applicable
_____ Community Building Department for Permits
         (sometimes requires 2 sets)
_____ Subdivision Committee, if any
_____ Total Number of Sets

**Blueprint Hotline**
**Call Toll Free 1-800-521-6797.** We try to process and ship every order within 48 hours. When you order by phone, please be prepared to give us the Order Form Key Number shown in the box at the bottom of the Order Form.

By FAX: Copy the order form at right and send on our FAX line: 1-800-224-6699 or 1-520-297-9937.

## Canadian Customers
### Order Toll Free 1-800-561-4169
For faster service and plans that are modified for building in Canada, customers may now call in orders directly to our Canadian supplier of plans and charge the purchase to a charge card. Or, you may complete the order form at right, adding 40% to all prices and mail in Canadian funds to:     **The Plan Centre**
                   20 Cedar Street North
                   Kitchener, Ontario N2H 2W8

By FAX: Copy the Order Form at right and send it via our Canadian FAX line: 1-519-743-1282.

## BLUEPRINTS ARE NOT RETURNABLE

---

**HOME PLANNERS, INC.**
**3275 WEST INA ROAD, SUITE 110**
**TUCSON, ARIZONA 85741**

Please rush me the following:
_____ Set(s) of Landscape Plan _____
      (See Index and Price Schedule)        $ _____
_____ Additional identical blueprints in
      same order at $10 per set.          $ _____
_____ Reverse blueprints at $10 per set.    $ _____

Please indicate the appropriate region of the country for Plant and Materials List (see map on opposite page):
- ☐ Region 1     Northeast
- ☐ Region 2     Mid-Atlantic
- ☐ Region 3     Deep South
- ☐ Region 4     Florida & Gulf Coast
- ☐ Region 5     Midwest
- ☐ Region 6     Rocky Mountains
- ☐ Region 7     Southern California & Desert Southwest
- ☐ Region 8     Northern California & Pacific Northwest

| POSTAGE AND HANDLING | | |
|---|---|---|
| **Carrier Delivery** (Requires street address—No P.O Boxes) | | |
| • Regular Service (Allow 4-6 days delivery) | $ 8.00 | $ _____ |
| • 2nd Day Air (Allow 2-3 days delivery) | $12.00 | $ _____ |
| • Next Day Air (Allow 1 day delivery) | $22.00 | $ _____ |
| Certified Mail (requires signature) If no street address available. (Allow 4-6 days delivery) | $10.00 | $ _____ |
| Overseas Delivery | Phone, FAX or Mail for Quote | |

*NOTE: All delivery times are from date blueprint package is shipped.*

POSTAGE (from box above)            $ _____
SUB-TOTAL                      $ _____
SALES TAX (Arizona residents add 5% sales tax; Michigan residents add 6% sales tax.)  $ _____
TOTAL (Sub-total and Tax)         $ _____

YOUR ADDRESS (please print)
Name _____
Street _____
City _____ State _____ ZIP _____
Daytime telephone number   (_____) _____

FOR CREDIT CARD ORDERS ONLY
Please fill in the information below:
Credit card number _____
Exp. Date: Month/Year _____
Check One:   ☐ Visa   ☐ MasterCard   ☐ Discover Card
Signature _____

## ORDER TOLL FREE
## 1-800-521-6797
## OR 1-520-297-8200

Order Form Key
TB38LP

# Helpful Books & Software

Home Planners wants your building experience to be as pleasant and trouble-free as possible. That's why we've expanded our library of Do-It-Yourself titles to help you along. In addition to our beautiful plans books, we've added books to guide you through specific projects as well as the construction process. In fact, these are titles that will be as useful after your dream home is built as they are right now.

## Planning Books & Quick Guides

| | |
|---|---|
| **TRIM & MOLDING** | |
| **33** | Step-by-step instructions for installing baseboards, window and door casings and more. 80 pages $6.95 |
| **PAINTING** | |
| **34** | Tips from the pros on everything from preparation to clean-up. 80 pages $6.95 |
| **ROOFING** | |
| **35** | Information on the latest tools, materials and techniques for roof installation or repair. 80 pages $6.95 |
| **WALLS & MORE** | |
| **36** | A clear and concise guide to repairing or remodeling walls and ceilings. 80 pages $6.95 |
| **FLOORS** | |
| **37** | All the information you need for repairing, replacing or installing floors in any home. 80 pages $6.95 |
| **PATIOS & WALKS** | |
| **38** | Clear step-by-step instructions take you from the basic design stages to the finished project. 80 pages $6.95 |
| **WINDOWS & DOORS** | |
| **39** | Installation techniques and tips that make your project easier and more professional looking. 80 pages $6.95 |
| **PLUMBING** | |
| **40** | Tackle any plumbing installation or repair as quickly and efficiently as a professional. 160 pages $9.95 |

**ADDING SPACE**
**41** Convert attics, basements and bonus rooms to useful living space. 160 pages $9.95

**HOME REPAIR**
**42** An owner's manual for your home. Sound advice on home maintenance and improvements. 256 pages $9.95

**TILE**
**43** Every kind of tile for every kind of application. Includes tips on use installation and repair. 176 pages $12.95

**WALLPAPERING**
**44** Use the book the pros use. Covers tools and techniques for every type of wallcovering. 136 pages $12.95

**BASIC WIRING**
**45** A straight forward guide to one of the most misunderstood systems in the home. 160 pages $12.95

**HOUSE CONTRACTING**
**46** Everything you need to know to act as your own general contractor...and save up to 25% off building costs. 134 pages $12.95

**VISUAL HANDBOOK**
**47** A plain-talk guide to the construction process; financing to final walk-through, this book covers it all. 498 pages $19.95

**CONTRACTING GUIDE**
**48** Loaded with information to make you more confident in dealing with contractors and subcontractors. 287 pages $18.95

**FRAMING**

**49** For those who want to take a more-hands on approach to their dream. 319 pages $19.95

---

# Additional Books Order Form

To order your books, just check the box of the book numbered below and complete the coupon. We will process your order and ship it from our office within 48 hours. Send coupon and check (in U.S. funds).

**YES!** Please send me the books I've indicated:

| | | | |
|---|---|---|---|
| ☐ 1:FH | $8.95 | ☐ 26:BYL | $12.95 |
| ☐ 2:BS | $8.95 | ☐ 27:ECL | $12.95 |
| ☐ 3:FF | $8.95 | ☐ 28:HPGC | $24.95 |
| ☐ 4:NL | $8.95 | ☐ 29:ARCH | $59.95 |
| ☐ 5:AA | $8.95 | ☐ 30:CDP | $8.95 |
| ☐ 6:EX | $8.95 | ☐ 31:CDB | $8.95 |
| ☐ 7:HPG | $12.95 | ☐ 32:CKI | $12.95 |
| ☐ 8:NES | $14.95 | ☐ 33:CGT | $6.95 |
| ☐ 9:AH | $9.95 | ☐ 34:CGP | $6.95 |
| ☐ 10:LD2 | $14.95 | ☐ 35:CGR | $6.95 |
| ☐ 11:V1 | $9.95 | ☐ 36:CGC | $6.95 |
| ☐ 12:V2 | $9.95 | ☐ 37:CGF | $6.95 |
| ☐ 13:VH | $7.95 | ☐ 38:CGW | $6.95 |
| ☐ 14:V3 | $6.95 | ☐ 39:CGD | $6.95 |
| ☐ 15:YG | $7.95 | ☐ 40:CMP | $9.95 |
| ☐ 16:DP | $7.95 | ☐ 41:CAS | $9.95 |
| ☐ 17:EN | $9.95 | ☐ 42:CHR | $9.95 |
| ☐ 18:EC | $9.95 | ☐ 43:CWT | $12.95 |
| ☐ 19:ET | $9.95 | ☐ 44:CW | $12.95 |
| ☐ 20:VDH | $12.95 | ☐ 45:CBW | $12.95 |
| ☐ 21:SH | $8.95 | ☐ 46:SBC | $12.95 |
| ☐ 22:WH | $8.95 | ☐ 47:RVH | $19.95 |
| ☐ 23:EP | $8.95 | ☐ 48:BCC | $18.95 |
| ☐ 24:ST | $8.95 | ☐ 49:SRF | $19.95 |
| ☐ 25:HL | $12.95 | | |

**Canadian Customers**
**Order Toll-Free 1-800-561-4169**

Additional Books Sub-Total $_____
ADD Postage and Handling $ 3.00
Ariz. residents add 5% Sales Tax; Mich. residents add 6% Sales Tax $_____
YOUR TOTAL (Sub-Total, Postage/Handling, Tax) $_____

**YOUR ADDRESS** (Please print)

Name _____

Street _____

City _____ State_____ Zip _____

Phone (_____) _____— _____

**YOUR PAYMENT**
Check one: ☐ Check ☐ Visa ☐ MasterCard ☐ Discover Card
Required credit card information:

Credit Card Number_____

Expiration Date (Month/Year)_____/ _____

Signature Required _____

**Home Planners, Inc.**
3275 W Ina Road, Suite 110, Dept. BK, Tucson, AZ 85741

TB38BK

# Index